Letters for Lucia:
8 Principles for Navigating Adversity
by David Brown Jr.

© Copyright 2015 David Brown Jr.

ISBN   978-1-63393-193-0

This is a non-fiction work intended as a real guide for helping others. To protect the innocence of the characters, fictitious names have been created to conceal their identities. The historical events, descriptions, dialogue and opinions are the sole expression of the author's imagination.

Published by

◣köehlerbooks™

210 60th Street
Virginia Beach, VA 23451
212-574-7939
www.koehlerbooks.com

Letters for *Lucia*

8 principles for navigating adversity

david brown jr.

VIRGINIA BEACH
CAPE CHARLES

Letters for *Lucia*

CHAPTERS

DEDICATION

Dear Lucia,

This book is dedicated to you. For the many months that we have been apart I have tried unsuccessfully to find "normal" because a large part of me feels incomplete. It helps to fill the void by viewing each day as an opportunity to make positive contributions to others. Though we've not been together in the same place and home and we've not heard each other's words and sounds, I feel your presence. You are constantly with me in my daily meditations and nightly dreams where I see your sweet smile and know that you are growing from a baby to a little girl. When I awake from dreaming of you, I am always glowing—so proud of how wonderful you are and happy to feel in this special place in my heart that you are growing and changing.

Many truly special friends, family members, and mentors have helped me to begin to heal and manage this time away from you. My heart is full of gratitude and appreciation to them, as you will read in the appreciation letters at the end of this book. I had a sense of being with you as I wrote this book and shared the important message that no one was at fault. Even though our circumstances are awkward, we are all trying to do the very best that we can. Our lives are constantly changing and rearranging, and despite our good intentions, we may make decisions that create pain for others and ourselves. While managing difficulties we often build new strengths. Through our moment-to-moment life experiences we learn new ways to more successfully navigate whatever comes next. You are full of love, and perhaps you are already helping others to understand.

Week by week I will continue to hand write letters to you until we are reunited. And this will be especially for you, my sweet, little baby girl. Though we are not living together every day, I want you to know who I am and who I was when you were born and who I have become since you came into my life. Writing to you and expressing my heartfelt story is my way of being with you and caring for you. I will always be committed to you, no matter what happens. You, my daughter, are the truest love I have ever felt. I am always sending you peace and love because you are the center space in my heart. It is my deepest desire that we will be reunited far sooner than we think, and for far longer than we ever imagined.

I love you always and forever,

Daddy

AUTHOR

David Brown Jr. is awakening to a compassionate heart and purposeful living. This journey began with sadness and chaos and the parental abduction of Lucia, his eleven-month-old daughter. In the anxious days following the abduction, David began writing notes to Lucia, and although he had no physical way to deliver them just putting pen to paper increased his heart connection to her. Encouraged by family, friends, spiritual teachings, and meditation experiences David very purposefully chose not to be governed by anger, and that choice initiated an overwhelming sense of compassion for his estranged wife, baby daughter, and himself. Since this book chronicles a true story, David has chosen not to use the real names of any individuals to protect their privacy and honor their wishes.

With new clarity David no longer saw himself as a victim and realized that he was being inspired by certain principles. His handwritten notes became Letters for Lucia and a vehicle for sharing the powerful principles that were redirecting his life: heart, awareness, intention, acceptance, compassion, loving unconditionally, forgiveness, and gratitude.

Regardless of contradictions or external circumstances, all of us have the unique ability to choose how we respond to wanted and unwanted things in our lives. We are choosing how to live, and the how's and what's of our choices profoundly shape our perspectives, paths, and potential for whole-hearted living in joy and peace. David and Lucia have not yet been reunited, but living in loving-kindness continues to be his focus toward Lucia, toward readers of this book, and everyone that he encounters.

PREFACE

A real and frightening experience
inspiring the most phenomenal shift
in perspective of my entire life.

*I*n November 2013 my wife fled the country taking our baby daughter with her, shocking beyond all my efforts to rationalize it. My wife and I had married only a few months before after a brief courtship, unexpected pregnancy, and tentative beginning of family life. A chance meeting on an evening out with friends brought us together and was made even more interesting by our different family and cultural backgrounds. I, nearly nine years her senior, am one of two children of an American, middle-class family and have lived, earned two college degrees, and begun my career in the northeastern U.S. The petite, dark-eyed young woman that I met that evening had only lived in the U.S. ten years, having relocated with her mother and brother from Uzbekistan when she was fifteen. She was working part time and going to college.

Our beautiful baby girl, Lucia, was born the week of Thanksgiving 2012. As wonderful and amazing as that was, it also initiated insecurities in our marital relationship, parenting confusions, and disagreements about finances. When Lucia was eight months old my wife and I agreed to live separately but jointly care for Lucia, she during the week and I during weekends. On one of the Saturdays that I was to get Lucia for the weekend, I received an e-mail from my wife telling me that she had gone away and taken Lucia with her.

After contacting local, state, and federal authorities and an attorney I found myself with little or no viable action to take. I reached out to many sources and advisors and persistently made inquiries. Although I have tried to reach my wife through numerous e-mails and texts, she has responded only three times, and I have no other means of contacting her.

Soon after that terrible day, a series of experiences and two distinct stories began to unfold that have changed my life as profoundly as my baby daughter's disappearance. Beginning small and swelling to larger and larger waves, I began to experience a personal, spiritual awakening. It registered so prominently that even amidst the chaos and mental challenges, I experienced an inner core of peace, and I began to flow real compassion toward my wife, regardless of the outcome of the situation.

Only days after they left I began to feel an urgency to write to Lucia, whom I desperately missed. There was no way to know when or how we would be reunited nor was an actual address known. Although Lucia was not old enough to read, writing the letters to her became an outlet for constant thoughts of her and a channel for my emotions. The profound shift in understanding that I have been experiencing has inspired me to identify a set of principles for leading a purposeful life and share them through daily letters to my daughter. This book, *Letters for Lucia*, brings together many of the letters, discovery of these principles, and aspects of my spiritual journey. These principles already exist within all of us. I celebrate the positive aspects that have been the focus of many wise teachers and masters, and I deeply appreciate the ways in which my fears and anxiety have been soothed.

Up until this trauma I have been very fortunate to have lived a calm and supported life. I was raised by loving parents, have a close relationship with my sister, and enjoy thoughtful family members and supportive friends and coworkers. From an early age I had great models for responsibility and values.

Initially, these chaotic circumstances seemed unnavigable and unimaginable. A number of months before meeting my wife I had been introduced to the practice of meditation and several spiritual philosophies. So I leaned on them, reaching for calmness, peace, and clarity. In my daily meditations, prayers, and general thoughts a greater good completely unfolded. The overwhelming anxiety and fear dissipated as eight principles came to me one by one. These principles—heart, awareness, intention, acceptance, compassion, forgiveness, loving unconditionally, and gratitude—formed a framework for living purposefully.

Expressed by great teachers and masters, many of these principles have been connected to well-known religions or philosophies. I've intentionally removed religious affiliations from this book, preferring to present to readers an open invitation to experience the principles as an enhancement to their own personal philosophies. I believe that this approach is truly powerful because it elevates our similarities. My hope is that once our similarities have been ushered to the front row, long-practiced judgments about dividing differences will fade away. Just imagine the joy that could happen if we all came together with a new emphasis on similarity! Incredible, peaceful experiences could be launched for all of planet Earth.

And in my opinion that mirrors the intention of God, Source, Creator—the name is unimportant, as the heart knows. Gradually, and profoundly, I have begun to live with a deep gratitude for all that had happened.

CHAPTER 1:
THE HEART PRINCIPLE

Seeking clarity about whether my mind
or heart is leading the way.

Dear Lucia,

Our hearts are like internal compasses, and I imagine that you, darling Lucia, are already feeling this special resonance. When I ignore my own heart messages it feels like resistance and not "being in the flow." In recent years I have learned to step back from actions or decision making, become still, and seek clarity about whether my mind or heart is leading the way. Each time I have done that, calm and clarity has prevailed.

Many times as I have approached decisions, small and large, I have recalled wise words from my own mother: "Follow your heart." It's with this sense of heartfelt openness that I've been able to become an alert, aware observer of the experiences of my life and the eight principles guiding me. All of us are life-long learners, and you especially are so new and naturally open, with amazing opportunities yet to come. A sense of togetherness moves through me as though I am talking with you as I think and feel these letters. In each letter I will share one of these eight powerful principles: heart, awareness, intention, acceptance, compassion, forgiveness, loving unconditionally, and gratitude. It is very comforting to imagine living these eight principles together with you. I am so happy to encourage you, as my mother has done for me, to live with an open heart and follow it to true freedom.

I love you always,

Daddy

Even though I was not initially awake to them, these eight principles for purposeful living were always subtly and consistently working in my life. Observing lack of forgiveness evokes desires for forgiveness and kindness. Discords, or contrasts, are great teachers and initiators. Remarkably, chaotic situations can reveal segments of stillness, the eye of the storm, where awareness is so powerful that profound meanings seem simple and natural.

In 1982, when I was about four and my sister was two, our family of four moved from northern New York to Delaware prompted by a layoff at the plant where Dad worked. Mom's identical twin already worked as a chemical engineer at the nearby refinery, and both Mom and Dad quickly found employment.

Since neither of my parents attended college, education was a big emphasis throughout my developing years. And it was a foregone conclusion, with no way to opt out, that my sister and I would graduate college. My sister was a triple threat, academically gifted, a star athlete, and beautiful. I was also academically gifted but too lazy to maximize my potential. In my early school years and through high school, I spent a lot of time playing video games and collecting basketball cards. However, when I began applying to colleges a wave of seriousness hit my academic life, and the bigger picture slowly unfolded.

I enrolled at a small, local business college with the intention of transferring to the University of Delaware in my junior year, which I did in 1998 as a finance major. That same semester I began working as a customer service representative in the financial services industry. Although juggling full-time work and full-time school was intense, I was determined to show myself and others that I could compete with my former peer group. A desire to prove myself was a motivator for years and years, both professionally and personally.

Time raced by after completing undergraduate school, and I had advanced to the position of vice president in financial services and sensed that I was on the threshold of coming into my own professionally. Then I segued into the professional services industry as a strategy consultant where my affinity for leading change initiatives advanced me further. After completing an Executive MBA at Villanova, I did some academic course development for their MBA program and was very fortunate to garner many exceptional professional experiences in a relatively short time period. In late 2011, a facilities management firm recruited me, and though it was a far cry from financial services, the focus of the job was strategic design and leading people through change. It was truly exciting that my career was flourishing, yet I had more room in my heart and yearned to fill the space.

I had always felt that a part of me was holding back while simultaneously eager to spring forward and emerge. This broader sense of self lay dormant for years, and I fumbled trying to articulate it—until 2012 when my life seemed to crack open and shift in new ways and with amazing speed.

During the time that I worked as a customer service representative in financial services I met Monroe who was a year older and more socially savvy. We accelerated one another's energy and quickly became best friends, close like brothers. On January 22, 2012 we were in Philadelphia and planned to go to one of our favorite places in Center City where bouncers, bartenders, and DJs knew us well.

The night was cold, and I was glad to be wearing a tailored pea coat with a cashmere scarf wrapped tightly around my neck. The cut of the black coat seemed to add inches to my six-foot-one-inch frame. As the bouncer checked our IDs Monroe and I shook hands with him and shuffled through the tall, glass entrance. Inside I surveyed the room and quickly noticed the familiar faces of Carla and Alicia, both former coworkers and recent college graduates. I knew Carla fairly well since I had actually been her team leader for a while. Smiling at both ladies, I boomed, "Hey, I know you!" Then I realized that a third lady stood between Carla and Alicia.

"This is my friend Jolie," Carla said.

I smiled and in a softer voice greeted Jolie, "Hello." Pivoting back to Carla and Alicia, I asked, "May I buy all of you a drink?" Still smiling, I moved away and walked with Monroe towards the bar.

The atmosphere fairly buzzed as Monroe and I elbowed our way through the crowd to find an open spot at the bar. The DJ shifted between current and classic, hip-hop and pop while sound volumes rose and random conversations escalated to compete with the music. The energy level was really high! I motioned to get the attention of Christina, one of the bartenders that I knew, and she nodded an acknowledgement as she rapidly poured and stirred cocktails. While I observed the busy bartenders, I heard Monroe's familiar and infectious laughter behind me. When I turned around I was eye to eye with Carla, Alicia, and Jolie. I moved a few steps to the left and waved them toward the bar as I handed them their drinks.

For the next few hours in a small space beside the bar the five of us talked, laughed, and became acquainted. Despite the rising noise levels in the club our conversations took on an intimate tone and a sense of closeness emerged. Jolie spent much of the night talking to Monroe while I quizzed Carla and Alicia about their career progress since we last worked together. When conversations slowed Monroe and I exchanged a familiar brother-to-brother nod, our signal to switch conversation partners. In a matter of moments I began talking one on one with Jolie while Monroe interacted with Carla and Alicia.

Jolie's petite frame was almost hidden by the three-quarter length, belted trench coat that she wore. Visible between the coat lapels was a very elegant, lacy black blouse topping dark-blue jeans and black boots. Her flowing black hair was held back by an ornate clip pressed against her scalp at the crown. As I moved closer to hear her voice, the bar's dim lights flickered across her face revealing eyes so deep brown that I could not distinguish between pupil and cornea. The hazy lighting created an exotic contrast with the fair, yellow hue of her skin, and I was instantly attracted, feeling a magnetic pull between the two of us word by word.

Jolie turned and seemed to position herself in a defensive way as I spoke. "Hello, again. How long have you known Carla and Alicia?" The very air between us felt stiff, as though we were playing a game, and I was boxed out.

"I met Alicia through Carla," she offered. "Carla and I have been best friends for a while. Both of us are from Uzbekistan and met when I moved to the United States with my family."

Intrigued, I responded, "That's interesting. So you are both from the same country, but met here. Which members of your family live in the U.S.?"

Jolie's discomfort gradually eased, and she began to talk more. "We moved here nearly ten years ago when I was about fifteen. My mom and brother are both here."

By my count that made her twenty-five, which was equal to the number of minutes that our conversation had been rolling. She was close to her small family and a student of international business at a local university. Her mother especially wanted to make the best of opportunities. Both of our families modeled working hard and insisted on good grades and education. I was impressed with Jolie, and even more so because of her association with Carla who I perceived to be an intelligent, talented young woman. When the evening ended, Monroe and I shared a seven-minute cab ride to his place during which I updated him on my conversation with Jolie. My desire to be loved and in love fueled my emotions. Monroe was a good barometer, and whenever I met someone new he kept me in check. But meeting Jolie felt very different.

The next weekend was my birthday, and I planned to celebrate by going out to dinner in Philadelphia. Nothing fancy—turning thirty-four didn't seem like a major milestone. The workweek progressed and thoughts of Jolie were ever present in my mind. On Friday I decided to send a text to Carla about my birthday dinner plans, inviting her to join me and to include Jolie. Surprisingly, Carla agreed and confirmed that she and Jolie would meet Monroe and me after dinner in Center City.

Over the next twenty-four hours I mentally entertained scenarios of how I hoped the evening might unfold. In my imagination Jolie and I exchanged phone numbers and agreed to stay in touch without any assistance from friends. On Saturday afternoon I shopped my own closet for the perfect shirt-jeans-shoes combination as well as a change of clothes to stay over at Monroe's. Then I eagerly drove to Philadelphia anticipating a long and happy night.

I enjoyed my birthday dinner with Monroe at a favorite Italian restaurant. Around 10:00 p.m. we headed for a nearby lounge and saw Carla and Jolie walking up the block toward us. We greeted one another with friendly hugs and made a quick decision to go somewhere to dance.

After several hours of dancing I found myself sipping water

at a bar, immersed in deep conversation with Jolie about goals, values, and family. Jolie had a strong desire for independence and defining her own personal success. That, in conjunction with wanting to be a loving wife and mother, was very attractive and reminded me of my sister, a mother of three who modeled our parents as she built her family and professional life in similar ways. My perception of the Uzbek culture was that family was the first priority, and I found myself thinking that the stars couldn't have been aligned any better. Our heavy conversation seemed out of kilter with the previous hours that had been filled with loud music and jumping. Yet it felt right and natural. For an hour we talked about our backgrounds and what we wanted to accomplish with our own families and careers. We were connecting. As 2:00 a.m. ticked by I was physically exhausted but emotionally and spiritually stimulated. I was intrigued by our conversation and eager to get to know Jolie and encouraged about having met someone with similar values about growing a family and having a successful career. Moreover, it was exciting to feel connected, something I had not felt in a long time. As the night ended we exchanged phone numbers. Meeting someone was something I highly desired, and a seemingly chance meeting unfolded it right before my eyes. The feeling seemed mutual as both of us were obviously interested in getting together sometime soon.

Our relationship heated up quickly, and in the first month we saw each other multiple times each week. It was easy to make time to see Jolie in Center City between her classes before I headed home from work. I was elated and felt a resurgence in my emotional energy as this heart connection began to take shape. We did a variety of activities together, including dinner dates and movies. At the end of our dates our connection deepened with stimulating conversations. At a very quick pace we were falling in love, and only a month into our relationship Jolie and I began discussing the possibility of marriage the following year, then starting a family. When you are falling in love it's easy to live in the clouds, however, on March 28, 2012 reality muscled in with a phone call from Jolie.

In a voice that was both apprehensive and worried, Jolie said, "David, I'm pregnant."

It was clear that she was concerned about how I would respond to this news. Somewhat stunned, I replied, "Okay." My mind raced and my breathing quickened. A first-time experience for me, I drew a complete blank on what to say. We were only a few months into our relationship, yet it was clear that I was in love with Jolie. Our hopes for a family, careers, values, and many other critical factors appeared to be aligned. We had argued a few times about minor things, but that was normal for any couple. I felt good about where our relationship was going.

"How do you feel about this?" I asked. It was important to know where her head was with this whole situation.

She answered, "I'm doing okay, and I feel good. But I am scared about telling my family."

I sucked in a huge gulp of air, feeling my lungs expand then pressing my diaphragm down with the exhale and swallowing the emptiness before replying, "What do you think your mom is going to say?"

Hesitation and nervousness were evident in her silence. Finally, she responded, "I don't know. I've never had this kind of news to tell her."

My attention diverted for a few moments as I gazed out the window of my suburban condo noticing that the sky was clear and the temperature cool. Then my thoughts sped up, careening like bumper cars at the fair, and I wondered what my very rational, levelheaded dad would say. I placed my warm palm on the cold windowpane and watched a shadowy imprint form and disappear in an instant.

"David, are you still there?" I heard Jolie's shaky voice on the other end of the phone.

"Yes, I'm sorry!" I said. "Let's go and talk to your mom together. I will pick you up after class. How does that sound?"

Jolie let out a long breath. "Yes, that sounds good. I will see you around 8:30 p.m. I love you!"

Before hanging up I said, "I love you too, babe! See you soon."

After picking Jolie up from school we experienced awkwardness and strained silence during the twenty-five-minute drive to her mother's place. Normally, Jolie would tell me about her classes or how much work she was doing on behalf of her study group. This evening she stared blankly out the passenger window unless I interrupted her silence peppering her with questions.

"What are you going to tell my mom?" she asked.

"Well, I've got a good career and think I'm in a position to be a father. So I'm ready for the responsibility," I responded. This circumstance was so new and somewhat of a shock. It had an eerie quality, like walking into a dark room, sensing something there, yet unable to see it. Before tonight we had only talked once about her pregnancy.

Nearing the apartment complex, Jolie used her cell phone to call her mother and advise her that we had arrived. I backed into a parking spot ready to turn off the engine. "Don't turn off the car," Jolie said. "My mom is going to come down."

In seconds I saw the shadow of a petite figure walking out of the main door of the apartment building. Jolie's mom, Ami, was very attractive, about five foot three and maybe 105 pounds. One of the first pictures that Jolie ever showed me was the two of them at a party—they could easily have been mistaken for sisters.

When Ami settled in the back seat behind Jolie I turned off the music and made a ninety-degree turn with my body to face her, a smile across my face.

With a slight Uzbek accent, Ami said, "Hello, David, how are you this evening?"

My nervousness was apparent as I spoke. I was uncertain about what to say or how to say it. "I'm doing well, and yourself?"

After exchanging quick pleasantries, Ami got right to the heart of the matter. "So Jolie has told you that she is pregnant. Is that right?"

"Yes, ma'am," I confirmed. Before Ami spoke I had assumed that I was the first to know and Ami would be surprised by what Jolie and I had to tell her. Then the conversation tilted, and I gradually understood that the question was to me, alone, as to my intentions and sense of responsibility for the situation. With the newness of our relationship it was natural for Ami to be protective of her daughter and to want to understand my intentions.

"So what is it that you want to do?" Ami asked.

"Well, I have a good job, and I love her. We should have the baby," I responded. Thinking that my response would please Ami I watched as her facial features morphed into sternness, and her shoulders raised and squared before she addressed me directly.

"In order to have the baby," Ami continued, "you must marry. In our culture, it's looked down upon for a woman to have a child and not be married."

I became a bit defensive. "I can appreciate that, but I don't think we're ready to get married right now. Since we've only been dating for a few months we should see how the relationship goes and make that decision later. I look at having a baby and getting married as two separate events. If you're saying that we need to get married in order to have a baby then I need some time to think about that. I can't make that decision right now at this moment."

My own values are firm, reinforced by growing up in a home where my parents taught that the ideal was having children after marriage. As I navigated my twenties, and the changing world around me, I observed more and more Western couples having children without being married. In my eyes, the key to the child's success was a loving environment and parents committed to ensuring the welfare of the child. I was very aware of some of the challenges my sister had faced as a single mother. Long before falling in love with Jolie I had placed in my heart a firm commitment to be 100% supportive and active in the life of future children, regardless of my relationship status.

Ami snapped back, "When will you be ready to make it?"

My nervousness traveled through my body, and I felt my stomach roll and my chest muscles tighten. "This is a lot to take in, a big decision. Honestly, I don't know." The words tumbled out. "I need a couple of days to think about it and talk more with Jolie to figure out our best options." Glancing over at Jolie I saw dismay in her eyes. She was clearly torn between the circumstances and respect for her mother and culture.

Shouldering responsibility and doing what was right always came easy to me. I certainly wasn't running but clearly needed time to think. Jolie and I both respected our parents and cultures, yet either choice would launch significant events in both of our lives. This was big, and my immediate response was to take some time to seek and understand my own feelings and sort through options.

Turning again to address Jolie, I said, "Babe, let's talk more tomorrow. I know we discussed getting married, maybe next year. Having a baby is one thing, getting married is very different. This is all happening so fast. I really don't think it's fair to make this decision right now."

My heart felt thicker and heavier as I perceived a sense of rejection from Jolie, which wasn't the case at all. Then Ami excused herself and left the car. Conversation became stilted and we only made a single decision, which was to speak the next day when Jolie got out of class. Clearly we held different perspectives, neither better than the other, just different. I was off from work the next day and going to Monroe's to facilitate delivery of his new television system. Moments later Jolie tearfully got out of the car, and I watched her walk up the three flights of stairs to her mother's apartment. Once I saw that she was safely inside I drove home, alone with my whirling thoughts.

In the morning, after a sleepless night, I called a few family members asking for their advice. I was confident that both of my parents would be supportive. Both told me that it was my decision to make, and my mother added, "Follow your heart." By 11:00 a.m. I was on the train, having arranged to meet Jolie at Monroe's place at noon.

Monroe lived on the second and third floor of a duplex located on the edge of a posh neighborhood in Philadelphia. Soon after I settled in the doorbell rang, and I made my way down the stairs to the main entrance to greet Jolie. I gave her a warm, loving hug as we walked into the small den and sat on the chocolate-brown, leather sofa. Sitting shoulder to shoulder we sensed one another's discomfort and began making small talk like casual friends catching up. Then, awkward silence.

After a few moments Jolie spoke, "So, what are you thinking?"

"You know that I love you very much," I said. "We have been together for such a short time, so I do have concerns about marrying so soon. We are still trying to figure each other out. Deciding to marry isn't something that I take lightly."

She drew back from me, repositioning herself on the couch.

Then she spoke, "In my country men marry women after only a few months of dating. If you truly loved me, you would be willing to make that commitment to me and our unborn child."

I didn't want to argue or judge whether one country's practices were better than the other. After all, I only knew the environment that I had experienced, which was also true for Jolie. We went round and round for about forty-five minutes, and then I verbalized my decision.

"I am willing to have and support a child, but not to marry at this time." I felt a sinking sensation in my heart yet continued, "They are two separate events. Once married, both of us would be committed to stay with it. But I am very committed to our unborn child."

Jolie looked stunned, and her tears began to flow. I put my arms around her and consoled her for what seemed like hours, pushing back my own emotions all the while. Here is a woman that I deeply care for who wants a child and wants me. Yet I appeared to be pulling both of those things away from her.

Thirty more minutes passed. There was nothing more to say, so we agreed to leave Monroe's and go back to our respective homes. After sharing a cab ride to the station, we sat in the terminal until the first train arrived. Apologetically, I kissed Jolie's forehead and then boarded the southbound train.

As the train traveled down the tracks the debate between my head and heart raged on, undiminished by the pulsing music streaming through my earbuds. What decision was the best one? How could Jolie and I even stay together if I did not want to be married? Hoping to slow my swirling thoughts and the world around me, I turned off the music and attempted to meditate. I began by focusing on my breath. Gradually the rapid-fire thoughts settled, and the sensory experience of the swaying train and passing countryside scenes took over. Then came the welcomed stillness. For a few precious minutes the intense feelings surrounding this huge life change subsided. And in stillness I realized two distinct views—a burning desire to love and be loved, and a painful fear of losing this new-found love. Adding financial obligations and responsibilities would be challenging in the short term. My thoughts jumped to concerns if things didn't work out and being able to be with the baby-to-be. But if I walked away from this love, would a connection like this ever come again?

As the reverie of the brief meditation ended, my mother's words from this morning's conversation came to mind, "Just follow your heart."

When I arrived back at my condo I walked to the kitchen, put my cell phone face up on the glass-top table, and sat down to stare through the window blind slats. For a few moments I made the phone spin by pushing the corners with my fingers, all the while imagining my jumbled thoughts falling onto the screen. Then I took a few deep, steady breaths, placed the phone in my palm, and initiated a call.

"Hello," I heard Jolie's sad and agitated voice rasp into the receiver.

"Hey," I said, "it's me. I am calling to check on you."

"Don't worry about me. I'm doing fine," she said with a tinge of sarcasm.

I knew that wasn't true so I continued, "Look this isn't an easy situation for either of us. I did more thinking on the train ride home, and I believe that we should try and make this work."

I sensed Jolie repositioning and pulling closer to the phone with a willingness to listen. She said, "What do you mean? What are you saying?"

I replied, "What I'm saying is that we should get married and have this baby together. I love you, and I think we should try and make it work. We're going to have a beautiful baby together. You're going to be a great mom, and I can't wait to be a dad. Let's chat a little bit later this evening about having a small wedding ceremony and making plans toward the baby's arrival."

Jolie's voice rose and brightened, "Are you serious? You want to get married?"

Hesitantly I responded, "Yes, I do. Go ahead and call your mom, and I will call my family to share the news." Her small family consisted of one grandmother, an aunt, an uncle, a few cousins, and her mom and brother. It was important for Jolie to be married prior to announcing a pregnancy, otherwise the family would've been ashamed. That became as important to me as it was to Jolie.

To the shock of my family and friends, I announced that

we were getting married on April 7th, only about one week away because Jolie's mom and brother planned to travel to Uzbekistan on April 15th. The ceremony took place at a small chapel in Philadelphia and was followed by a dinner with family and close friends at a local restaurant.

The Heart Principle

Every time my mother's words, "Follow your heart," came to mind I experienced calm and clarity. Focusing on my heart space and feeling my way through the mental commentaries netted different results than analyzing and "statisticalizing."

Fear was my initial response when Jolie first told me that she was pregnant. Although we had not been together very long the logical side of my mind had imagined step-by-step progress where we would develop our relationship and consider marriage and future children. In my thoughts I sorted marriage and divorce statistics, friends' precarious relationships, and even a few TV show examples. Mental models and scenarios came and went, often leaving me uncertain about making a good decision.

The loving side of me was very excited about the possibility of having a family. Though it was a road I hadn't traveled, it was a responsibility that I looked forward to and embraced. Watching my parents sacrifice so much to provide for my sister and me initiated my own desire to experience a rich family life, as well as having a strong personal and professional foundation. My sister also modeled that behavior. Taking a leap and following my heart seemed eminent, and once my fears subsided I felt that I was on the verge of creating that harmony.

As I progressed from my twenties to early thirties my reliance on logic and objectivity (the head) began to shift toward values and subjectivity (the heart). Answers derived in academia often appeared very black or white. My shift from head to heart was already in motion as I transitioned from academia to the working world. When I applied theoretical models in new professional experiences I gradually realized situational influences and areas of gray and the rarity of anything completely black or white. Led by my heart, I exercised more intuition and openness to gain broader understanding. What an amazing new way to experience the world! This was very far removed from what I had previously practiced and had observed in others.

Today I endeavor to live in this heart space, open to possibilities. I am in touch with my true feelings and keep judgment and mental traps at bay. It has become easier and easier to rely on my internal compass and check for my "true north." When I am off course I can feel resistance like the water flow of a stream blocked by fallen tree limbs. With that awareness I mentally position myself as an observer and step back from individual situations, which allows me to determine whether my mind or heart is in charge. By no means am I saying that all of my decisions have been 100% right since the moment I began leading with my heart. We live in an ever-expanding universe where information, resources, things, and people constantly evolve, as do opportunities to learn and grow. I deeply appreciate continuing to learn, grow, and shift perspectives. If your desire is to expand, as mine is, I sincerely encourage you to pursue true freedom by quieting your mind and opening your heart.

The reflection questions at the end of each chapter are designed to allow you to begin thinking about how the principles can be applied to various areas of your life. My suggestion with any self-exploration exercise would be to take your time to digest the question and understand what shows up for you in terms of answers. Some answers may show up right away, while others may take time to manifest. Be gentle with yourself as you move from one question to the next.

The following reflection questions are related to
the Heart Principle:

R | Who has influenced you to follow your own heart?

E
  | What happened when you did—or didn't?
F

L | What does intuition mean to you?

E
  | What is your signal to yourself to make
C | you aware that you are aligning with your "true north"?

T

I | When that signal shows up how does it feel?
  | Is it a sound? Does it have a color?

O

N

S

CHAPTER 2:
THE AWARENESS PRINCIPLE

Gaining understanding about who I was
and who I wanted to become.

Dear Lucia,

I hope that you will be able to do your best to be aware and present in each moment. Sometimes life events and circumstances move so rapidly that you may feel like you are running just to keep up. When you are running to get somewhere or playing a game with a friend, it is easy for your active body to take over, going and going like a machine. If a gate or a rock appeared in the road you might shift your steps so easily that you had no conscious awareness of the physical change. Those types of responses are often ruled by emotions, such as fears of stumbling and getting hurt. One of the most wonderful things about you, and all thinking beings, is the ability to make choices. The choices you make and responses you evoke are truly the only thing you can control since circumstances and other people are beyond our control. Your potential is unlimited, and by practicing mindful awareness you will also become undefined by emotional responses that others may make. As your confidence for making choices grows so will your levels of awareness, becoming the lens through which you perceive the world and all of your wonderful experiences.

I love you always,

Daddy

Things were moving very rapidly, leaving little time for Jolie and me to question our fluctuating definition of normalcy. The prior summer I had purchased a condo, and we planned to live there for at least a year after the baby was born. Jolie's family relied on the income from her part-time job, so we agreed that Jolie would live with her mom and attend school during the week until the baby's November due date drew closer. During the week she lived with her mom, went to school, and worked. We were together on the weekends, which seemed like a good transition although not ideal for a newly married couple. Her schooling continued, her family was supported, and I began saving for a second vehicle. I had concerns about Jolie's family's ability to manage without assistance once Jolie stopped working, however, we clearly separated my finances from her family's financial plan.

Since Jolie's mother and brother were going to Uzbekistan a week after our wedding, we agreed to take care of the two cats and house-sit for the two months they were away. Their apartment was located in the heart of a predominantly Russian community, about forty-five minutes north of my condo. On a Thursday afternoon Franklin and Ami flew to Uzbekistan, and I arrived on Saturday evening, ready to begin married life with Jolie.

I lugged my two suitcases up three flights of stairs, caught my breath, and lightly knocked on the door. A few moments later my beautiful wife opened the door. "Come in and put your bags down," she exclaimed, glancing down at her apron. "I'm making us dinner. Come to the kitchen with me." Her smile spread from ear to ear and she was glowing, clearly glad to see me.

Exposing my purple-gray-and-black argyle socks, I slipped out of my shoes and carried both bags to the master bedroom where I was greeted by two cats walking quietly toward me. One was black with piercing green eyes, and the other was a brown and cream mix with a beautiful fluffy mane; Siamese I presumed.

Pointing first to the Siamese Jolie said, "That's Primo, and the other one is Athena." The black cat rubbed against my right calf and began to purr. "We've had them for several years; they are part of the family."

Jolie took my hand and led me into the kitchen. "Follow me, babe. I'm almost finished cooking."

The smell of ground beef, coriander, and cumin pulled me forward. When it came to food all of my senses came alive, and I spent a lot of time in the kitchen experimenting with different flavor profiles. For years the Food Network and ESPN were my favorite TV-viewing options. To show off my own cooking skills, the day after our wedding I made my favorite dish for Jolie's breakfast, challah-stuffed French toast.

"Whatever you are making smells fantastic!" I said. On this special evening I was very happy that she had prepared our first home-cooked dinner together.

Her smile widened as Jolie explained, "These are Russian cutlets. We fry them in a pan and serve with rice."

The little patties reminded me of small meatloaves, and the preparation appeared to be the same, except these were fried rather than baked. Periodically, Jolie checked a large pot of rice on the back of the stove. After ten more minutes of eager anticipation, dinner was ready. As a self-proclaimed foodie, I was very impressed with Jolie's skills. Everything was fresh, appealing, and very tasty. We topped off the meal with a hot cup of green tea.

Sipping the hot tea, Jolie announced, "This is really good for digestion."

"Really?" I responded. "I've never thought about tea aiding in digestion. Before today I only drank hot tea in the morning or when I had a cold or with a dessert. It makes sense."

A little smile flickered across her face as Jolie nodded and refilled our cups with hot tea. After we finished, Jolie shuffled me into the living room while she cleared the table. Since I had been single and living on my own for eight years I was accustomed to and took pride in cleaning up at my own place. This time Jolie insisted that I relax. After a few minutes she joined me on the couch to talk.

About eight feet away and parallel to the kitchen table a brown, faux-suede couch and love seat rested while an isolated, over-stuffed chair stood near the entrance door. We got comfortable on the love seat and began talking about her mother and brother's trip. Although life in the United States offered many more opportunities and amenities, pride and love for Uzbekistan ran deep within her. When Jolie spoke of her homeland it was as if it was a long-lost parent. That night we sat for hours viewing her laptop screen as Jolie narrated hundreds of digital pictures of the country and its beautiful sites. I felt my initial nervousness about being married quickly transform into a peaceful calm because everything about the evening was extremely inviting and comfortable. Our evolving connection was what I had always hoped for, and our bonding felt very natural. From my vantage point, our future together and starting a family was clear and bright.

It only took about two weeks to map out a routine for the sixty mile daily commute, which took about ninety minutes round-trip. My job was fairly new, I was newly married, and was living in an unfamiliar place. The new job as a senior leader at a facilities management firm was a far cry from financial services where I had worked the previous fourteen years. It was a great opportunity to help lead a smaller organization through strategic change, which is what I'd always desired to do. To shorten the learning curve I needed to devote forty-five to fifty hours per week to the new job. When I was working, Jolie was equally busy balancing classes, assignments, and a part-time administrative assistant job. Regardless of her busy schedule, she always ensured that our "home" was immaculate and that we enjoyed a home-cooked meal every night. I remember thinking, "How did I ever get so lucky?" This was the type of life that I had hoped to have with her. Even though the surroundings were unfamiliar and I was away from my own family, Jolie did a really good job of folding me into her element, and I became more and more comfortable living in her family's apartment.

In mid-June Franklin and Ami returned from Uzbekistan, and I moved back to my condo where Jolie would stay on weekends. For two full months we had been living together as a married couple, so shifting to only two days a week seemed like a big step backwards. Regardless, we made it work, and our time together became that much more special.

Through summer and into the fall, I couldn't have been any happier. I was becoming very comfortable helping my new organization improve operations, although concerned about their financial positioning. Both families were very excited about our new addition. When we learned that the baby was a girl, we immediately decided to name her Lucia, which means light. We both thought Lucia was a beautiful name. When we dreamed about our future and a second child, we envisioned choosing a first name from my side of the family. Love and excitement about our new addition flowed from both families, although they had only come together for the wedding and a surprise baby shower for Jolie, which was planned by my mother, sister, and Jolie's best friend, Carla. Both future grandparents sent regards and asked about each other all the time.

On Labor Day weekend of 2012, Jolie moved in and settled with me and continued her fall semester classes. I purchased a second vehicle so that she would have independent transportation. As November approached everything was ready for Lucia's arrival. We set up a crib, changing table, and dresser in the large bedroom where we slept. Even though our one-bedroom condo was only 660 square feet everything fit fine and never felt cramped to me.

Things shifted again when Jolie began living with her mother in mid-November because the hospital where Lucia would be born was only fifteen minutes away. While out shopping with her mother on the evening of November 25, 2012 Jolie called me at home.

"Babe!" she shouted into the receiver. "I think I'm in labor right now!"

Immediately filled with excitement and nervousness, I heard Jolie's short, panting breaths and sensed that they were very different from the Braxton-Hicks contractions she had experienced during the previous four weeks. "Don't worry," I reassured her. "I'll leave here and come right to the hospital to meet you."

She responded, "You better hurry!"

I literally jumped from the living room to the bedroom and grabbed the bag already packed for this special day. In one swooping motion I pulled a coat from the closet and slid into my brown, leather loafers. Then I darted to every electronic device ensuring that they were turned off and secure and lastly checked the thermostat. The next time I saw this place our precious baby girl would be with me. I raced down the flight of stairs, pulling on the edges of my disheveled, unzipped jacket. Not even allowing for car warm-up time, I peeled out and left skid marks on the cold parking lot pavement of the quiet condominium community.

The two-lane road leading to the highway barely seemed wide enough as I rushed past cars on the left and right of me. Though a small part of me favored caution, I ignored the 55 mph speed limit signs, easily hitting 75 mph until I reached the suburbs of Bucks County. Normally a forty-five-minute trip, thirty-five minutes later I wheeled into hospital parking.

Guided by signage and memories from our birthing classes, I ran through the hospital hallways toward a bank of elevators. I lurched inside an elevator and impatiently rode to the third floor. Stepping out into the waiting area I smiled at the bold green letters, *MATERNITY*, painted above double doors leading into the secure reception area. When the receptionist asked for identification I nervously fumbled with my wallet and gave her my driver's license.

"Mr. Brown, please come this way," she said heading down the corridor and pointing to the third door on the left. I was instantly aware of ringing and beeping monitors, a large room, a large bed, four women, two nurses, Jolie, and her mom. To avoid Lucia being impacted by any drugs Jolie had insisted on an all-natural childbirth, which I supported. Yet seeing her in pain and hearing her screams, I was immediately uneasy.

Tossing my coat across the back of a chair, I asked a nurse how I could help. The elder of the two nurses told me to wash my hands then directed me to feed ice chips to Jolie between contractions and to hold one of her legs. Nervously, I leaned over Jolie, kissing her forehead, then patted sweat beads on her forehead with a cloth. "It's going to be okay babe, you're doing a great job!" I encouraged.

"Ahhhhhhhhh... ," she screamed as she continued pushing. The exhaustion of thirty minutes of pushing contorted her face, and her head rolled down onto the bed. For the next twenty minutes I fed teaspoons full of ice chips between her parched lips and into her mouth. With each contraction Jolie appeared to pull from a deep well of motivation to deliver our baby girl. Twenty minutes after my arrival the crown of Lucia's head appeared, and the doctor made final delivery preparations. A few more strong pushes occurred, and I was full witness to the miracle of life as my daughter's tiny body was pulled from Jolie's. The doctor asked if I wanted to cut the umbilical cord, a significant rite of passage for new fathers. Afterwards, I watched intently as the nurses cleaned and swaddled Lucia. Although I had heard crying babies before, these were the most beautiful sounds I had ever heard and absolutely distinct. Crossing the room to Jolie's side, I kissed her on the cheek in gratitude. When Jolie held Lucia for the first time I saw their two faces glow with both joy and relief.

Post-delivery, a peaceful calm blanketed the room. While Lucia was being examined and monitored by the nurses and Jolie rested, I called my family and used my phone to send the first photos of baby Lucia. The joy in my parents' hearts was evident as they sent welcoming messages to their fourth grandchild. Since my sister was due any day, there would soon be a fifth grandchild. The next morning my parents visited us in the hospital sharing their full excitement for Jolie and me. As mom and dad both held Lucia for the first time their excitement and joy was obvious.

Forty-eight hours later Jolie and Lucia were discharged to come home. I had taken two weeks off from work to be home with Jolie and our little angel. Since she was not working at that time, Ami volunteered to stay with us for the first week, helping us acclimate to becoming parents. It would be a tight fit in our small condo with three adults and a newborn, but how difficult could it be?

For me, becoming a first-time parent was nerve-racking in many ways. Although many people said that you just end up figuring it out, I felt completely unprepared. Jolie had read a multitude of books throughout the pregnancy, and I had absorbed information through our conversations and birthing classes. I was amazed by Jolie's strong sense of knowing what to do and growing confidence bolstered by Ami's guidance. There is no doubt that Lucia's birth was a joyous occasion, but our first few weeks of family life were far less smooth than I had hoped.

Ami helped in so many ways—cooking, cleaning, clothes washing, and anything Jolie needed. Relegated to observer, I felt pretty useless but was extremely appreciative. Ami moved so quickly to accomplish everything that needed to be done that I had trouble keeping up. I often asked if I could assist but was usually too late. Even for middle-of-the-night feedings I was helpless because Jolie nursed Lucia. Each time Lucia cried all three adults woke up. If it was feeding time Jolie fed her then Ami would take over burping and diaper changing. Then Jolie would put her back to sleep. My confidence quickly shrunk; doubtfulness expanded and I became irritable. Although Ami gave her best efforts, my defense mechanisms rose each time she attempted to teach me basic baby care. It was reminiscent of being a teenager and receiving instructions from my father. Back then I thought that I knew it all and explanations were a waste of time.

Images of being that kid flashed by when Ami calmly said, "No, David, lift her legs up this way to change her diaper. Use your other hand."

"I got it!" I snapped back. "I know what I'm doing!"

Then Jolie would rush to her mother's defense. "David, do it like my mom says. She knows what she is doing!"

"Well I know what I'm doing, Jolie," I announced.

The faces of both mother and daughter mirrored displeasure and disappointment at my unwillingness to listen. Soon my doubtfulness turned to exclusion, and I made it known that I did not welcome someone coming into "my house" and telling me what to do. Unfortunately, both mother and daughter heard my curt responses and witnessed my withdrawn body language.

After a chaotic week in the small condo Ami decided to leave the following Saturday. I drove her home and we endured an awkward silence upon reaching her apartment. The tension from the week was evident, and neither of us really wanted to talk. I made an attempt to dispel the tension in the air. "Thank you for all of your help. I know that it wasn't an easy week for you, or us. But thank you."

"You are welcome, David," Ami responded then grabbed her bag, closed the car door, and walked toward the stairwell of her apartment building.

When I arrived back home Lucia was asleep in her crib, and Jolie was sitting on the couch reading on her iPad.

"Hey," I said closing the front door and opening the closet to hang my coat. No sounds came from her voice, but her facial expression transmitted a clear message. I eased into the leather recliner directly across from her, waited a few moments, and then asked, "What's the matter?"

Jolie placed the iPad on the couch, straightened her back, squared her shoulders, and fairly shouted, "I can't believe how you disrespected my mom this week! She has only been trying to help us. You refused everything that she had to offer. You really didn't know anything, but you acted like you knew everything. I'm so pissed off, David, so ashamed of the way that you treated her."

My heart sank as I processed Jolie's words and emotions. "Was I really that bad?" I thought. Or was Jolie's close bond with her mother raising her sensitivity? Either way, she had every right to feel the way that she did. And I couldn't deny that I had been an ungracious host and an unwilling learner when Ami had only tried to teach me how to properly care for my newborn daughter.

Later that evening I went for a drive by myself to clear my head and do some shopping. When I left, Jolie and Lucia were both sleeping peacefully in the bedroom. Sitting in my car in the parking lot of the local organic supermarket I called Ami. Her phone rang three times before she answered.

"Hello," I heard her soft voice on the other end.

"Hi, it's David. Have I called you at a bad time? Were you sleeping?" My words were halting. "I just wanted to speak with you for a moment."

"No, I'm okay, David," she responded.

Cautiously, I began, "Okay, I just wanted to call and apologize for the way I treated you last week. I didn't realize how much I may have hurt your feelings by not listening to the things that you were trying to tell me. This is such a stressful time, and I let it get the best of me. So I want you to know that I am truly sorry and completely appreciate all that you've done for us."

Ami took a deep breath, digesting the sincerity of my emotional words. "Thank you for calling to apologize, David. I know that the birth of a first child can be very stressful and challenging for both mother and father. Understand that I only want to help both of you become very good parents."

Hesitantly, I continued, "I know you do, and I really am thankful for your help. It's been a long week, so I hope you get a chance to rest. We will call if we need anything."

"Okay, David, goodbye." And she hung up.

After the conversation my heart felt lighter, but I knew I still had a long way to go to rebuild Jolie's trust. And I had even more to learn about caring for my daughter. Once the grocery shopping was done, I picked up fresh flowers to surprise Jolie. My hope was that I would soon be on the way to making amends.

The Awareness Principle

As I observed the transformation of my wife's body and emotions, I was enormously aware and awed by this life-creating space. It was as if my shoulders had suddenly been shaken, and the jolt clarified that my life experiences were no longer going to be singular. Soon I would have direct accountability for the development of another human being, significantly amazing in itself, and a responsibility larger than I had ever imagined.

During the two months that Jolie and I house-sat for Ami, I experienced strong feelings of isolation. Except for clothing, none of my personal things were there. My parents and sister, with whom I am fairly close, were at least ninety minutes away, and I rarely saw them. Since our house-sitting assignment minimized disruption of Jolie's work and school and only lasted for two months, I didn't resist. Yet fatherhood's fast approach raised significant questions in my mind and heart. My desire to understand surged forward and my hunger deepened. Always intrigued by symbols and deeper life meanings, I eagerly sought scholars and books on spirituality and metaphysics and embraced meditation as an important part of my daily life.

Although I was new to meditation, I quickly experienced many changes and strong feelings of comfort and peace for which I yearned. I just simply felt better after each time of meditation. Even though Jolie and I had few disagreements prior to the week after Lucia's birth, when disruptions occurred my place of solace was meditation. I chose to meditate at the beginning and ending of each day when my wife and daughter were sleeping, and I focused on quieting my mind and "being." Over time my meditative states grew deeper and more profound, and a more intense knowing unfolded. I gained understanding about who I was and who I wanted to become.

Early in my career I observed the types of actions that more successful leaders were taking to get ahead. I was attentive because I, too, wanted to reach a certain level of achievement. In the early 2000s, my motivation was strictly financial, aimed toward wealth creation and living a particular lifestyle. Progressing into more senior roles, I led larger groups and my influence on the well-being of people began to emerge. With the beginning of my meditation practice came a deeper, wider understanding about leadership skills, the impact on people, and how natural and authentic the process was to me. Sometimes my pride and habits of behavior would tug on my thoughts and lure me back to old ways of thinking and being. However, I was intent on becoming a truer me, and after each meditation I always emerged in a very accepting and neutral state of being, and everything was "clear."

As my meditation practice deepened, my sense of self began to transform. I often reflected on responses to past situations, such as the conflict between Ami and me. I recalled rebelling against my parents during adolescence and emotional outbursts when I resorted to shouting if things didn't go my way. When I remembered arguments between peers or friends I realized that my responses had been emotional and judgmental. Like assembling puzzle pieces, an outline formed, and I discovered that agitated emotional responses did not occur when my mind was clutter free. When I focused and was just "being," a sense of neutrality prevailed. No matter what the circumstances were prior to meditation time, when the meditation concluded agitations had dissolved. So my inner voice asked, "Do I choose my emotions?"

What a profound discovery! I gained full realization that I am completely in charge of my emotions and the ways in which they do or don't define me. I am the one, the only one, choosing how little or how long I hold on to wanted or unwanted emotions. Most importantly, all of my emotions come directly from me—some on the surface, others from a hidden reserve. When something occurs in my environment that triggers painful feelings, unchecked I may respond defensively.

We often judge or label someone else's emotional response as "good" or "bad." But when opinions and emotions have been cleared away, an emotional response is neither good nor bad, it just is. Many of us send out negative, or lower, energy as a defense mechanism or form of self-protection. Did you ever have a classmate in elementary or middle school who regularly lashed out in class, bullied others, or instigated trouble? Maybe you kept your distance from that child but later on learned that he or she had a difficult home life, felt unloved, or was neglected. You may be friends with or have coworkers who have chosen to carry negative feelings for decades, perpetuating suffering in their day-to-day lives.

Deepening meditation experiences have significantly expanded my awareness, through which I now understand emotions to be conditioned responses. When we repeat certain actions or emotions again and again we form habits from those practices. The "doing" is a type of conditioning, which is demonstrated in our responses. The "doing" is not intelligent in and of itself. Verbally or non-verbally we assign definitions (labels) to everything around us. Therefore, we have ultimate choice in the how, when, and why of our emotions. Generated internally, they don't define us; we define them.

Imagine that everyone and everything happening around you is assembled in a fast-moving, rushing river. Emotional responses naturally occur as we bump into and collide with one another in the rush of this river of experiences. Consider people with whom you interact, routinely or in single instances. How would you describe their navigation methods? Are they pushing against or flowing with the current? If we removed all of the "ifs," "ands," and "buts" we would find that most of the time everyone is truly trying to do their best. What if we gradually awakened to the genuine knowing that we are only able to control our own individual responses and not circumstances? We would gain great clarity about the origins of our own responses, as well as expressing empathy toward others responses. I believe that mindfulness would increase exponentially! Shifting from agitated outbursts to empathetic observations will fuel compassionate understanding. It's equal to turning on a light in a dark room.

As we travel through life our experiences are our profound teachers. Parents, other adults, and siblings introduce our immediate environment and the order of it. Very early on, and from many different sources, we are introduced to guilt, shame, and embarrassment as well as happiness, joy, and gratitude. In the situation that I described with Ami's week-long visit, my response was similar to a knee jerk or patellar reflex. The behaviors that I exhibited were rooted in early childhood experiences and practiced so continuously that they seemed almost rote. Having a well-meaning Ami trying to teach me something new during an uncertain, anxious time was equal to having a doctor's rubber mallet hit my tendon. I am especially glad that I had already begun the practice of meditation because my irritable response to the first week of parenthood, well-meaning instructions, and our crowded condo helped me to really understand conditioning and the power of awareness.

If I could have gazed through a two-way mirror and observed those experiences from a distance it would have been fairly easy to recognize their commonalities: my own feelings of fear, insecurity, and angst. When Ami, an experienced mother and eager grandmother, began to "tell me what to do," my response may have been like "teenage David," all the while insisting that I was an adult with the right to choose. What was really powerful for me was seeing myself through Jolie's eyes then making a direct apology to Ami and honoring the needs of my own inner child. For many of us, myself included, defensive responses, anger, or feelings of isolation are attempts to shield our inner child and vulnerability.

Throughout my growing-up years my father did his best to get me to explore the world and try new things. Fueled by fear or general unwillingness, I resisted many invitations, yet my father insisted that I ride roller coasters, play certain sports, and try other activities. As a child I wasn't even remotely open to enjoying those experiences. I didn't understand and often responded with resentment. Now, as an eager explorer of deeper meanings and awareness, I understand his intentions but will endeavor to do differently.

By strengthening my own awareness, I can now respond to my environment very differently. The composite of all of our myriad experience significantly influences our moment-to-moment decision making. And during the times that we enter into situations unaware of the origin of our emotions, or unresponsive to others' emotions, our responses may well be knee-jerk, autopilot-like. Without having made a definitive choice to be alert and aware, past conditioning is likely to preselect a default response. Meditation has not only raised my awareness levels, but it has also helped me to recognize past decisions made through default responses. Since everything happens for a reason, I don't go back and debate or agonize over past decisions that could have been made differently. However, as my self-awareness continues to transform, I am purposefully ensuring that I am completely present and in a non-emotional state of being when making choices now and going forward.

The following reflection questions are related to
the Awareness Principle:

R What new "awareness" have you had this week or month
E about the impact of your behavior on others?

F If you were more aware of your emotions how would
L your life improve?

E
C How would you describe the manner in which your
closest friends or family members are navigating their
T rivers of experience? Are certain people on "autopilot"?
I How does that show up?

O Do you tend to bring people up to your emotional energy
N level, or do you tend to drop down to their emotional
energy level?
S

What is your experience with mindfulness?

CHAPTER 3:
THE INTENTION PRINCIPLE

Becoming aware of perceptions
and setting positive intentions and allowing
them to be anchored in my heart space.

Dear Lucia,

Our thoughts are very powerful, even for one as young and sweet as you are. We show our family, friends, and the world our thoughts by the beliefs and behaviors we express. We live in an attraction-based universe where "like attracts like." So that means that when we share positive thoughts, we attract more and more of the same. And when we demonstrate negative thoughts and behaviors, we attract more of the same. Some people become overwhelmed by their environments and perpetuate unhealthy patterns. But I believe in your innate wisdom and that you won't get stuck in that way of thinking and being. If you will always try to be aware of your perceptions, set positive intentions, and allow them to anchor your heart space, it will be natural for you to do good for yourself and for others. That deep knowing will direct you toward a path of always giving and receiving loving-kindness. In my heart is the intention for us to be together very soon.

I love you always,

Daddy

I wanted to ensure that the family I was now building had a solid support system, so in February 2013 I suggested that we leave our condo and move to the apartment complex where Ami lived. Though it moved me further away from my parents, sister, and friends I believed it would eliminate Jolie's sense of isolation from her family and friends. Despite changing our living situation, and making compromising a priority, nothing seemed to work for Jolie and me. The tension that developed the week after Lucia's birth, and Ami's stay, lingered like the smell of stale cigarettes. Our biggest point of contention was Lucia's healthcare, and co-parenting became more and more challenging and frustrating.

When Lucia was about three months old she was diagnosed with a mild form of torticollis, a neck condition. It took our pediatrician more than two months to finally make a diagnosis, whereas Jolie realized it when Lucia was about two weeks old. Fear that the condition would worsen and growing frustration with the healthcare process put Jolie on edge. She took Lucia to a local children's hospital for physical therapy, however, the twisting/turning neck exercises were too painful for Jolie to watch. After a few sessions Jolie proposed an alternate solution.

"Babe, Lucia's condition isn't getting any better," she began. "And I think we should find another treatment route."

Hesitantly, I responded, "What did you have in mind?"

"Well outside of the U.S. there are other alternatives." Jolie paused. "They could help our little Lucia get the treatment she needs. I was thinking that we could..."

She didn't have to continue because my immediate response would emphasize that we were only a thirty-minute drive from one of the best pediatric hospitals in the world. I anticipated her rebuttal and felt myself drawing inward.

Since Jolie avidly researched babies, babies' health, and interacted with other mothers online she experienced other influences. "We could go to Moscow or Uzbekistan. I have done some research on their treatment approach for torticollis, which combines infant massage with physical therapy. Lucia would be relaxed and her muscles would be warmed up before work on her would begin."

"No," I interjected. "I don't understand why you feel that

local treatment options are not good enough."

"They twist and turn her around. She cries the entire time," Jolie began, raising her voice. "They are painful for Lucia, and I won't take her there anymore."

The tone of my voice grew stern. "We must figure out something else, Jolie. This seems extreme, and we can't afford it." In the back of my mind I wondered whether Lucia's crying during treatments had more to do with being touched by strangers. She was very hesitant with new people but always soothed by Jolie's comforting voice and touch.

With a piercing stare Jolie said, "You and your money! It's all you ever worry about. Do you want to have a crippled daughter? That will happen if you don't do something about her neck."

Without even taking a breath I snapped back, "You don't get it! You think we have all of this extra money floating around, and we don't. We are on a limited budget. And yes, of course, I want to do what's best for Lucia. We just need to explore realistic options. Sending her out of the country is not on the table." I found myself speaking to Jolie like she was a business client. "We must figure out how to make our finite amount of resources work for Lucia's good. Her condition is not so rare that we can't get treatment here. I know that it is taking time and you are frustrated with the healthcare system. So please let me help to work through it. We will find someone local who can help."

Jolie turned away and scooped Lucia up from her play mat on the floor. "You don't care about me or Lucia. All you care about is yourself!" With a finalizing glance she stomped into the bedroom and slammed the door.

I rubbed my forehead from side to side and realized that my face actually hurt from using my muscles to squeeze together brows, eyes, and cheeks. Rarely have I ever had a complete blowout with someone, and I felt a discernable sense of relief that the argument was over. The tension, disappointment, and anger I was holding in my physical body was like a rope tightly bound and stretched from forehead to toes. Alone in the living room, I pondered all that had been said. Was I not being heard, or was I not hearing Jolie? It was probably both. Sinking into the couch cushions I didn't feel unreasonable, but rather misunderstood. I loved my daughter dearly and would do anything for her. The options Jolie had laid out felt very unlikely to me. I haven't seen many things that doctors in the U.S. can't do. At the same time, I did not for one minute discount the importance of treating Lucia's condition. A part of me held onto our pediatrician's estimation that Lucia's torticollis was mild and she would grow out of it. However, Jolie was alarmed about a worst-case scenario. I turned on the TV and aimlessly scrolled through multiple channels until I fell asleep on the couch. Jolie and I didn't speak at all the rest of the night.

It seemed like we avoided eye contact and conversation for the whole of the following week. Jolie and I prepared separate suppers, yet we sat at the table together and during playtime with Lucia. She sat at the table to feed Lucia while I ate. Once Lucia and I had both eaten, I got on the floor with her for playtime while Jolie cleaned the kitchen and prepared Lucia's evening bath. To an observer it would have all seemed very fluid, yet the communication void for a newly married couple made for an uncomfortable time. I could feel that our union was unraveling. Our frequent arguments increased a sense of cohabitating and diminished our marriage. The only positive was that as long as we weren't talking, we weren't arguing.

One evening after Lucia was in bed, Jolie and I sat on opposite ends of the couch and she brought the subject up, again. "What are you going to do about Lucia's treatments?"

Surprised by her question, I defensively replied, "What do you mean what am I going to do?"

Somewhat challenging, she replied, "Well are you going to send us out of the country for treatment?"

"Haven't we already settled that question?" I answered. "I have not changed my mind. We need to figure out something else."

Our argument continued, and the twenty minutes we spent defending our respective positions seemed like an all-night affair. If Jolie was unwilling to accept treatment for Lucia at the local pediatric hospital it seemed that I had no other solutions to offer. Tired and out of responses, I said, "If you cannot find a local treatment that will work then we can discuss sending Lucia away."

The tension in Jolie's face eased and she appeared pleased.

The deepest part of me didn't like anything about what I had just said. But I really wanted to stop arguing and bring things back to calmness. And for the rest of the evening the tension between us disappeared. In the moments before I fell asleep I worried. "What if Jolie's worst-case scenario was correct and Lucia's condition was more severe?" I would be the one to blame for slow response to treatment. I even asked a pediatrician who is a good friend to consult on possible treatment methods. He explained that infant massage treatment protocols didn't really exist in the U.S. To get that form of treatment Lucia would have to receive care outside of the country. After a few days of researching options, Jolie and I sat down to discuss the details. Beyond the expected health benefits for Lucia, I was optimistic about Jolie feeling better and our return to functioning like a happy family. Now it seemed that taking Lucia to Uzbekistan was the better approach because healthcare costs were less expensive than Moscow, and some of Jolie's relatives still lived near the capital.

Jolie completed Lucia's passport paperwork, and I had a letter notarized authorizing a visa for Lucia to be out of the country from late May until the end of July. We hurried to make the travel arrangements, and within a few weeks Jolie secured an apartment. Jolie, Lucia, and Ami, who would accompany them, planned to stay with Ami's sister and family for about a week until the apartment was available.

A week after Lucia's passport and visa were approved they left the States. The total cost of the trip was $15,000, and I ended up borrowing most of it. The money covered Jolie, Ami, and Lucia's transportation, living expenses, and healthcare costs.

I missed my family terribly and hated coming home to an empty apartment. Two days after they arrived in Uzbekistan I was very relieved to receive Jolie's telephone call and to learn that my family was safe and everyone was doing well. I hoped that we would be able to chat via Skype so that I could see them, especially Lucia, but their limited Internet access and time zone differences made consistent communication difficult. Jolie and I phoned a few times every week so that I could get an update on Lucia's treatment schedule. Periodically during our calls, she would put the phone to Lucia's ear, and I would sing to her just like when she was here at home with me. The combination of infant massage and physical therapy was an aggressive approach, but after a few weeks Jolie seemed pleased with the results. Sensing her relief eased my anxiety as well. Jolie said that the doctors in Uzbekistan questioned why she had not brought Lucia to them sooner, however, Jolie responded somewhat vaguely so as not to reveal that she and Lucia lived in America. Lucia was nearly five months old when the treatment began, so the doctors advised Jolie that Lucia would require extended therapy to ensure the cure. We became uncertain as to whether two months of treatment would be sufficient.

While home alone I focused on work, and evenings and weekends I delved deeper into compelling desires to explore more aspects of meditation. As if I had activated a signal, people began to come into my life who practiced the same positive energy that I was developing. In a very short time span I had cultivated a new network of friends who were eager to share their understanding of meditation and other spiritual practices. I met energy healers and Qi Gong practitioners and many new people who lived all aspects of their lives from this heart space of loving-kindness. My openness and desire to understand brought a crowd of people willing to share their experiences and explore knowledge.

I found myself completely embracing the idea of the universal connection of everyone and everything. Lucia's birth was probably the trigger point of my desire to understand how and why we create life. Jolie and I each had intense bonds with Lucia, not often spoken but palpable. I was experiencing the world as wondrous, and my fascination increased my openness to experiences and ideas that I might have ignored or avoided in earlier years. The natural unfolding and expansion continued as I began reading the works of authors such as Eckart Tolle and Michael A. Singer. I recorded episodes of Oprah's *Super Soul Sunday* and the fascinating speakers because their views and the subject matter stirred me deeply. Suddenly, I felt like I was "getting it."

In June my friend Sean introduced me to a Reiki master named Susan. Our first telephone conversation lasted ninety minutes, and I was intrigued enough to commit to her Level 1 Reiki course the following Saturday.

Susan lived about twenty-five minutes north of our apartment in a serene and comfortable development populated by light-blue carriage homes, majestic old trees, and dense shrubbery. Everything about her radiated a warmth and energy different from any I had ever felt. An abundance of synchronicities just seemed to be calling me and leading toward new people, spiritual teachings, and practices.

When Susan asked me how my interest in Reiki came about I replied, "Meeting you and coming here I'm hoping to gain more clarity about what's going on with me."

"It sounds like you are right where you're supposed to be," Susan responded. "Your awareness of these sensations is a good thing, David. I encourage you to continue to follow your instincts whenever these physical or emotional experiences occur."

Susan handed me a small workbook of Reiki materials, which further fueled my eagerness to learn more. The lesson began with Susan sharing the history of Reiki and elements of the practice. After a short lunch break Susan gave me my first-ever Reiki session, which took place in a room dedicated to her healing practice.

At the beginning of the session Susan asked if I would like to set an intention to receive something specific during this session. The idea of setting a specific intention was completely new to me, so I asked Susan to guide me.

She took a few steps toward me and spoke, "Setting your intention is like dedicating the session to something and putting it out to our universal guides to be revealed to you. It could be about your body or people or situations. Just focus, and something will come to you."

I nodded, smiled, and immediately thought about the health of my baby girl and the state of my marriage. An intention came to me, and I said, "Susan, I would like for my intention to be toward the greater good unfolding for my family." Just stating this intention gave me a warm and comforting feeling.

Throughout the session I experienced small flashes of light and several dreamlike scenarios. In one dream I watched myself and Lucia playing in Center City, Philadelphia in Rittenhouse Square. She appeared to be four or five years old and was riding a tall, pink bicycle with streamers waving out of the ends of the handlebars. Jolie wasn't with us, instead another woman who wore a brown, leather jacket and had blonde hair. There was little to distinguish before the scene shifted to an older Lucia, perhaps ten or eleven. We sat at a kitchen table smiling at each other, and I was helping her with homework. I felt Jolie's presence, but not in the kitchen.

When the session concluded it took me a few seconds to really pull myself together and respond to Susan, "That was incredible. I don't even know what to say. I actually feel very light and refreshed. How do your other clients describe it?"

Susan told me that Reiki practitioners usually receive visions or messages that are supposed to be shared with recipients. "David, there's no way for either of us to confirm for the future, but I feel that more will be revealed to you as time progresses. Sometimes the messages I receive immediately make sense, other times they seem to be disguised and take more time to unravel. My best advice is to just continue to be open to receiving whatever comes as your journey unfolds. But I will say that your level of awareness is higher than many people I meet who are just beginning to seek deeper meaning in their lives."

After lunch Susan taught me about the seven chakras and led me through a visualization exercise to attune these energy points within our bodies. Although I was being introduced to so much so fast, something about it felt very intuitive, like an inner knowing.

Then it was my turn to practice what Susan had demonstrated, and she invited her husband Anthony to join us in the Reiki room where she guided me to deliver an abbreviated session to him. When the session ended his response was incredibly positive. I glowed with amazement, and Susan smiled with encouragement, proud of her new student's first lesson.

With this new level of awareness, over the next few weeks I began to notice changes and subtle variations in my personal energy. A small quarter-inch space in the center of my forehead periodically tingled, sometimes so intensely that it mimicked a headache. At the time I didn't know if it had any meaning or connection with Reiki, so I just acknowledged the feelings and continued doing whatever I had been doing to encourage becoming more aware and open.

One month after my initial Reiki lesson with Susan, Jolie, Ami, and Lucia returned from Uzbekistan. Our time apart and Lucia's marked improvements seemed to have smoothed the rough edges of our family relationships. I had missed them very much and was excited that my family was home. That night Lucia seemed especially tired from the trip, so we played for only a short while before Jolie swept her off to bed, a little earlier than usual. Then Jolie and I spent time talking about Lucia's treatments and their experiences during the trip. And I told Jolie about my deepening and satisfying meditation practice as well as my first experience receiving and giving Reiki. The practice of Reiki piqued Jolie's interest because she had been experiencing pain from a mild form of scoliosis.

"Would you mind if I tried giving Reiki to you?" I offered. "I haven't had a chance to practice on anyone except Susan's husband, Anthony."

"Sure, that would be cool. What do I need to do?" she asked.

"When we go to bed I'll just place my hands on your back and will offer you Reiki that way," I responded, and she agreed.

Sometime later when we went to bed I lay in my normal spot closest to the door and asked Jolie to lie with her back towards me, on her side, facing the bedroom wall. "You don't have to do anything but drift off to sleep as you normally do," I said. "And I will just rest my hands on your back through the night." Then I placed one hand between her shoulder blades and the other about halfway down the middle of her back. "Is that comfortable for you?" I asked.

She nodded and we both relaxed. Before I dozed into sleep I set my intentions to stream healing Reiki energy toward Jolie.

In the middle of the night I awoke and my hands were still pressed against Jolie's back. When morning came Jolie awoke very refreshed, even after yesterday's seventeen-hour overseas flight and two-hour drive from the airport. "How's your back today?" I asked.

"Actually, it feels really good. Whatever you did worked!" she replied. "I woke up in the middle of the night and felt an amazing warm glow all over my back. Then I realized that your hands were still on my back. Thanks so much, babe!" she exclaimed and kissed me softly on the lips.

Nearly a month later Jolie told me that on a daily basis she had continued to experience a warm sensation of two hands touching her back. She said that it was very comforting and seemed to alleviate her sporadic back pressure. Although my understanding was limited about how the Reiki energy was working, it was clearly very positive for both Jolie and me.

The Intention Principle

Intentions are fueled by individual thoughts or emotions. Each intention carries an energetic value, which influences outcomes—regardless of whether it was ever verbalized or written. In my opinion intentions are among our most powerful tools.

If I define an oncoming situation as problematic even before the event occurs, I have created a perception, a perception of difficulty. In the moment that the "difficulty" label forms in my mind an attitude is also shaping. An attitude is almost directional, the way we turn to face something or the intention we have toward it.

Here is an example to consider. One weekend in 2014 after a West Coast business trip, I visited a friend in San Francisco. Over dinner my friend expressed deep concerns and asked for my opinion on rapid changes in the world and terrible acts taking place. Unfortunately, unkindness and injustice is disbursed globally, but my friend's examples all referenced where Lucia is likely to be right now. For a few minutes we talked about impacts on broader humanity, and then my friend's intensity raised as she posed more questions.

"What about all of the horrendous acts that have taken place all over the globe in the past fifteen years?" she charged. "Surely someone should come in and stop all of these groups that are harming so many people," she said.

"What outcome are you hoping to create by squashing those groups?" I asked.

She turned and looked out the restaurant windows, thinking for a moment before responding, "Ultimately, peace should be created for everyone in all parts of the world."

"I agree with you 100% on desirable outcomes," I said. "But, for me, how to go about it and actions to take are the complete opposite of what you have said." The puzzled look on my friend's face encouraged me to say more.

I continued, "Force plus force agitates and increases imbalance, and the intention behind that type of response emanates from negative or lower-level energy. That type of wipe-it-out, forceful action is not generated from peaceful, hopeful intentions. Of course, aiming for widespread peace is an ultimate goal, however, beginning with a barrage of negativity is unlikely to substantiate it. Instead, I feel that we should encourage positive change through compassionate actions. Unfortunately, many people are suffering and some have exerted power over others in an attempt to protect themselves and gain a semblance of control."

I smiled and continued, "When anyone whose focus is on universal love happens to encounter a negative situation, the intentions that they previously set are far more likely to be positive and inspire others. At first it may seem more difficult to purposefully endeavor to see others through kindness and compassion. However, as more and more people make the connection between compassion and valuing each individual, breakthroughs will come much faster, and previously dominant negativity will evaporate."

I took a slow, deep breath then continued, "Don't get me wrong because I'm not saying that this is easy or would happen quickly. To break down masses of negative conditioning could take generations. Or, or, or... the possibility exists that it could work like a line of standing dominoes—when the first one is tapped it leans into the next one and next one in an impressive continuation. A significant shift occurs as more people release negative influences and embrace peaceful, positive ones followed by more humane, sustainable outcomes. I have never been a very political person, but I think this could apply to governments and political parties. However, my feeling is that as long as groups and populations focus only on winners and losers and the belief that only one group's interests will be accommodated, an unwillingness to find middle ground will continue. Yet when individuals and groups are inspired toward well-being, it is highly possible for new realizations and positive shifts to rapidly occur. Through collaborative idea exchanges everyone's needs can be met rather than the limited, restricted outcomes resulting from devaluing others and disrespecting different set of interests."

A smile crept slowly across my friend's face, acknowledging that the concepts I had shared were percolating in her mind and heart.

Since we are the ones in charge of our perceptions and attitudes, we definitely have the power to change them. However, we must first become aware that we created them on our own and that they are impermanent. An intention toward an outcome forms once we have defined a perception and taken a stand (attitude) on it, such as, "I intend to slog up the hill and knock down that difficult situation." Many of us have formed the habit of labeling things we think about as good or bad. What if, rather than affixing judgmental labels, we envisioned thoughts as energy frequencies that varied in higher or lower registers?

Influenced by wise teachers, loving family, and spiritual thinkers I have eagerly delved into my own thoughts and the intentions behind them, embracing the practice of mindfulness. What does it mean to be mindful? It means to be very attentive to thoughts as they come and go, experiencing them objectively without labeling them as either good or bad. The ability to truly appreciate each present moment deepens through self-understanding, and in so doing, we become alert to and aware of influences on our thoughts and their temporary nature.

When I am centered and mindful my ability to stop and reform my perception rises even before an intention is fully shaped. My revised perception might be, "This situation may test me, but I am okay with that. And I know how to ask for assistance." Just that small perception revision could have a significant influence on the next version of my intention, which might be formed like this, "I intend to give my best effort and to feel good about seeking assistance."

All of us are born with the power to form and shift our perceptions and intentions toward outcomes—all, not just a few. Most importantly, one individual inspired to project positive intentions can influence a shift in perceptions for an entire group, which may launch positive outcomes for everyone concerned. It is my hope that reading these words and examples will inspire a desire to begin practicing mindfulness with your own thoughts and become more alert to your perceptions and flow of intentions.

As a result of my Reiki experience and deepening meditations, I began to have a much broader understanding about the power of intention in all of us. A year or two before discovering meditation or Reiki I would have instantly dismissed anyone who told me about alternative healing methods or focused intentions. But my experience was clear—it can and does happen when there is openness and sincere belief in the possibilities. My first Reiki experience was amazing, and I have continued to explore and study it, which has deepened my understanding of how we send energy into our immediate environments and to the world through our intentions.

Our intentionality is so powerful that it can single-handedly shape how you experience life. As intentions flow outward, your perception is shaped and reshaped by the feedback of your experiences. Here are some reflective questions to get you thinking about how your intentions impact you every day.

The following reflection questions are related to
the Intention Principle:

R
E
F
L
E
C
T
I
O
N
S

If you have an upcoming project or a goal, what was your intention about it yesterday? How has your intention changed today?

When you approach a situation that may not feel so comfortable, what are your intentions about the outcomes? Is there an alignment between what you were thinking and what actually happens?

Do you feel that you are in charge of your perceptions? Why? Why not?

How often do you sit and ponder your intentions and the outcomes you want to create in your life? Are there areas of your life that could benefit from positive intentions?

What are the special actions that you take to center yourself?

CHAPTER 4:
THE ACCEPTANCE PRINCIPLE

When being overly critical of yourself, or when your
self-image is distorted, it becomes difficult to express
compassion or acceptance toward others.

Dear Lucia,

You are going to be enjoying so many wonders and beautiful experiences as your life unfolds. Along the way things may happen that neither you, nor I, would be able to make sense of or understand. There are aspects of life that many of us try to control, so it is wise to recognize that we only have control over ourselves and our responses to our immediate environments. When someone is impacted by the actions of another they may even feel an urgency to reach out and take charge of what is happening. In those types of situations our sense of self, or self-image, may push forward trying to label things right or wrong, good or bad. Our self-image is often referred to as the ego. Since we experience consciousness through our egos, it is incredibly important and beneficial to create a kind and accepting relationship with our own ego. If you are overly critical of yourself, or your self-image is distorted, it could become difficult to express compassion or acceptance toward others. We are all part of a larger, universal order that is constantly unfolding, and it is my hope that as you grow you will want to learn to be nonjudgmental of people and things that may not be immediately understandable. To come to a place of acceptance does not mean giving up or giving in. Instead, it means to become more allowing. As things and events unfold around you it is easier to develop this feeling of allowing when you reduce emotional attachments to outcomes. The fewer judgments you place on others, the more you will grow in compassion and trust for the unfolding universal order. Gradually, you will realize that others are doing the best that they can moment by moment. By holding a sacred space for compassion and making acceptance a daily practice you will support and expand your own inner peace. Attachments to what is happening or to controlling outcomes will gradually become unimportant, and you will feel radiant living your life.

I love you,

Daddy

"The only thing that is constant is change" is a statement attributed to Heraclitus, an ancient Greek philosopher. In the warm, secure feeling of having my family back home, playing with Lucia and being amazed at her development, I entertained the hope that all immediate challenges had been met. Little did I know that the most dramatic sequence of events of my life was about to unfold.

Within one week of my family's return from Uzbekistan, Jolie suggested that they go back for continued treatment of Lucia's torticollis. She knew how much I had missed Lucia and the large amount of money borrowed to fund the first trip, so I was shocked that she was asking so soon after coming home. Lucia was seven months old when they returned home, and I had missed two entire months of her life and watching her grow. Internally, I began to feel excluded by the family I was attempting to create.

My unwillingness to borrow another large sum of money for a second trip out of the country led to continuous arguments with Jolie. It is not in my nature to quit anything that I have committed to without giving a solid effort and seeking middle ground. I made several suggestions to Jolie about meeting with a marriage counselor, but they were not welcomed. So much had taken place over eighteen months, and we reached a point where both of us just wanted relief from the tension. Each wanted a new sense of balance, but separately.

Towards the end of the summer and into the fall semester when Jolie returned to school, our relationship deteriorated very quickly. Jolie moved back in with her mother, and Ami became Lucia's primary caregiver during the week when Jolie was in class, and I worked full time. The arrangement ensured that Lucia's caregiver was always a close family member. Because of my long commute to work and Lucia's early bedtime I was not able to see her much at all during the week. So we had agreed that Jolie would bring her to me on the weekends. On a cold October evening Jolie and I decided that it was best to continue living apart and that we would begin planning to file for divorce at the end of the year.

Jolie intended to return to work at the end of the fall semester so that she could contribute more to living expenses with Ami. We agreed to share custody of Lucia so that we both could be a part of her life experience. I expected to provide financial support to cover Lucia's expenses. We seemed to be agreeing in theory, but on November 3rd Jolie and I had an extended argument via e-mail. She wrote that her intention would be to run up larger legal expenses for the divorce to which I responded that I would seek full custody of Lucia. Although our e-mail exchange was very emotional, going for full custody of Lucia was an idle threat on my part. I never imagined dire repercussions. Jolie and I didn't communicate for several days, which was for the best because we both needed to cool off.

On the morning of November 9th the severity of the situation climaxed. I was at my parents' home making a quick stop when I heard the chime of an e-mail notification on my phone.

Jolie's e-mail began, *"Hi, David, I want you to sit down and take a deep breath before you continue reading this letter…"*

An invisible rope seemed to circle my body even before I read the next sentence. Reaching for my glasses with one hand and moving the screen of my iPhone closer with the other, I felt the rhythm of my heart skip and my throat muscles clinch.

Jolie's words on the screen continued, *"I know that it is still early, and you are probably wondering where we are. I have taken Lucia and we have gone away. I took Lucia with me because I couldn't live in fear any longer knowing that I could lose her one day. As her mother I could not live my life without my only child."*

The digital clock on the television cable box reported 9:30 a.m. Just five minutes earlier it had appeared to be a routine Saturday morning. I had driven to my parents' home before a haircut appointment and planned to return to my apartment in time for Jolie to bring Lucia to me for the weekend. Now the skin on my neck prickled and my breathing quickened. Sweeping the iPhone screen with my thumb I scrolled quickly through sentences, rushing to absorb words and meaning. Jolie and I had been experiencing communication and marital problems, and three weeks before we had begun living apart. Although pinpointing our issues would be difficult, they accelerated soon after our daughter Lucia's birth last November.

The e-mail concluded with these terrible words, *"Lucia will be raised with peace, love, and care. Once she grows up, I will tell her who you are. And she will make the choice to find you or not when she turns eighteen."*

Never would I have thought that she would leave and take Lucia away. Was this nightmare really happening? For an instant I considered slamming my phone against the nearest wall in hopes that the message would just disappear. Jolie and I both have done some immature things to get under each other's skin at times, but this threat was beyond comprehension. I tried calling her then shot a simple text message, "Call me. Where are you?" that was followed by a text and telephone call to her mother. Neither responded.

Meanwhile, I heard my father pacing back and forth in the kitchen and talking on the phone. His tone indicated that something was wrong. But I was frozen in the living room, stunned by Jolie's message. Then I became aware of the sound of his footsteps, the foyer closet door opening, and the rustling of keys. I headed for the kitchen, eyes fixed on my iPhone screen, continuously thumbing through Jolie's frightening message. My face must have mirrored my anguish.

"What's wrong?" my father said.

In a barely audible voice, eyes still glued to the small screen, I said, "Jolie took Lucia!"

My dad barked out, "What do you mean?"

It took every ounce of my energy to hold back tears and just say, "I don't know! I'm still reading her e-mail. But I think Jolie took Lucia." It is not my habit to lie, let alone to my parents. I just didn't know what to say, even after reading the e-mail three times.

Over the past year he had been father, coach, and counselor to both Jolie and me and by all appearances was very invested in our marriage working. A truly special man, my dad makes everyone feel that he has their best interest at heart. For a moment I expected him to ask me to sit down and talk about what was happening. He did not offer that this morning but instead said, "Your mother just called and Aunt Varney is experiencing complications." This was unexpected news, and my heart sank as Dad said, "I'm headed to the hospital."

Before I could take in what was going on with my aunt, my phone rang. I hesitated before viewing the caller ID, anxious that either Jolie or her mother were returning my messages and ready to reveal their whereabouts. But the phone screen displayed my sister's name, leaving me somewhat relieved but extremely anxious.

Placing my ear to the phone, the first sounds I heard were my sister's sobs and then, "I just got off the phone with Mommy," another sob, "Aunt Varney—the hospital is trying to revive her." My thoughts whiplashed into place as I listened to indiscernible words coming from my sister. I was speechless, no longer registering the meaning of words. Unable to focus, I merely responded with, "Okay, okay, okay." Then I slowly disconnected the call.

Disjointed thoughts about a haircut and errands flickered through my mind as I walked from kitchen to garage to car and felt the slight shake of metal-on-metal door closing and then inserted key to ignition. Alarming thoughts snapped together— my wife had abducted my daughter; my aunt was dying! My father and I sped away in separate vehicles having agreed to meet at the hospital.

The drive to the hospital was the longest ten minutes of my life, further constrained by a barrage of inner dialogue prompted by Jolie's shocking e-mail. Did she really take Lucia? Where would she go? What if I am not able to see Lucia until she is eighteen? Am I a bad person? What went wrong for my aunt? Just yesterday she was dealing with pain management but recovering well from surgery. Was she going to be okay? How would my family hold up through all of this? When should I tell everyone about Jolie and Lucia?

Rolling into a space in visitor parking, I tried to calm myself by gulping deep breaths and squaring my shoulders. Through the windshield I could see my father 200 yards ahead, so I exited the car and quickened my pace to catch up with him.

A large, glass revolving door signaled the visitors' entrance, and to the right of the doorway was an imposing wooden desk flanked by a tall, metal stand displaying the words *CUSTOMER SERVICE*. A smiling, blonde-haired woman wearing a knit sweater embellished with the hospital logo greeted us, "Good morning, how can I help you?" After my father explained that his sister-in-law was a patient and that we wished to join family already here, the woman politely directed us to the main elevators, wing 3C, and the family waiting room. Dad offered to wait in the lobby for my sister who was on the way while I headed for the third floor where Mom and Aunt Dee Dee were waiting.

Exiting the elevator on the third floor I saw the word RECOVERY printed on a large, green sign. Then I rounded the corner and saw a wall plaque with an arrow pointing toward the family waiting area. The woman's directions had been easy to follow, and I entered a large, pleasant room where a small, wall-mounted television was tuned to local news. Other than muffled voices coming from the television set the room seemed eerily quiet. I spotted a wooden-arm, padded chair in the right hand corner positioned next to a lamp table. From there I had a full view of all coming and going, but for now, I was alone in the uncomfortable quiet.

After a few minutes a tall, slender woman with blue eyes, fair skin, and grayish hair came in and introduced herself as the hospital chaplain. Although it seemed odd, the chaplain said that my mother and aunt would be out shortly. Five minutes later my mother led the way when she and her twin, Aunt Dee Dee, appeared. Their demeanor was solemn with eyes red rimmed and cheeks tear stained. Mom swallowed several times then fumbled her words, "She... she didn't make it." A deep, sharp breath sucked through my ribs, held for a few seconds, and then surged out through my nostrils. My stomach twisted as I said, "What happened?"

"We don't yet know all of the details," Mom explained. "Yesterday there were some issues with managing her pain, but today she was doing fine. We don't know—it could have been a heart attack or a stroke."

Everything in the room seemed to tunnel backwards as I sank into the wooden-arm chair, my eyes filled with tears, and all edges turned fuzzy. It felt like I was under water. Then my mother's arm stretched across my shoulders, comforting me like a warm sweater. After a few moments of small gasps and sobs, Mom and Aunt Dee Dee composed themselves enough to begin making phone calls to their four siblings to let them know about Aunt Varney's passing. I marveled at their compassion, courage, and strength. Shortly after watching Mom make her last call, I saw my father and sister making their way down the hall. My sister and I are very close, and it deeply affects me to see her in pain. To cover my feelings, I turned away while my parents broke the news to her. When I returned my sister's face was buried in my father's chest, and the locked arms of my parents and Aunt Dee Dee formed a ring of support around her. My sister and aunt were especially close, and my aunt was godmother to my nephew. I made my way into their huddle just long enough to kiss my sister on the forehead. Then I edged toward a window that framed the fading sunlight of early afternoon skies and struggled to make sense of the events of the morning. The fluctuating emotions of this day left me unable to discern between intensities—my dear aunt's death and the abduction of my daughter. So many questions sliced through my thoughts... why am I experiencing this? And why now?

After family and friends had been notified of my aunt's passing, I decided to go home to sort through Jolie's message about leaving with Lucia. First, I went to my apartment to confirm that no one was there, and then I walked across the courtyard to my mother-in-law's place where Jolie and Lucia had been staying. Six months earlier I suggested that we put our condo up for rent and find a place closer to Jolie's mother. Mother and daughter were close, and Lucia being the first grandchild, I knew that my mother-in-law wanted us to live closer to her. As I walked the 600 feet to Ami's building I scanned the parking lot, but there was no sign of my mother-in-law's car. Taking the stairs two at a time I reached the third floor. Before raising the handle on the door knocker I cupped my ear to the door, listening for movements inside the apartment. Silence.

I pounded the door knocker three times and anxiously listened for any movement. Then I knocked three more times, exerting enough force to cause the neighbor to look out his door. No response from apartment 3E. On the third try I gripped the knocker handle with my left hand and the door knob with my right. To my surprise the door was unlocked. I slowly pushed it open and eased into the room, uncertain about the legality of entering yet indifferent to consequences. The living room was a wreck with white garbage bags full of clothes and other debris clumped between the couch and living room closet door. Quietly making my way around, I saw the brown, synthetic-suede couch, loveseat, and chair resting in their normal places. Lucia's brand new high chair sat in the kitchen, and a few remnants of food led me to believe that she had been fed before they left. I rapidly opened and closed drawers and cabinets, glancing at my mother-in-law's few remaining dishes. In the bedroom bags of trash sat on the floor and the bed. If it were not for Jolie's e-mail I would have feared that a robbery had taken place. Closets and dresser drawers were completely void of clothing or mementos; nothing of Lucia's remained. Deflated, I backtracked through the rooms, locked the front door, and walked back home. Calling the local police was my next step.

Ten minutes after calling the local police station there was a loud knock on my apartment door accompanied by a bold voice announcing, "Police!" I opened the door to two officers, one middle-aged with a gray mustache and his partner, younger perhaps by fifteen years. I invited them both in, and the older officer faced me and talked while the younger partner walked through the apartment assessing where and how I lived. When I retold the events of the interview I recalled that my father said during interrogation or questioning officer observations contribute to evaluating credibility.

"So what happened with your wife, Mr. Brown?" the older officer began.

Comfortable with his demeanor, I responded, "We started living apart three weeks ago, and our daughter spends weekends with me. This morning I received an e-mail from my wife stating that she had taken our daughter away. It appears that her mother is also with them. I tried calling and texting both but have not established contact. I'm guessing that their phones are turned off since both of their numbers go straight to voicemail."

The younger partner's small notebook waved back and forth as he gestured and moved closer to me for his next question. "Any idea why she would take your daughter and where they might be?"

"Jolie's e-mail states that she feared losing custody of our daughter," my voice broke before continuing, "and didn't want the agony of the divorce process. I'm not sure where they could be because they don't have any family in the U.S. They have friends in New York City and could have gone there... or they could have left the country."

"Is your daughter a U.S. citizen?" the senior officer asked.

"Yes, yes. She was born right here last November," I responded.

The officer continued, "Well, they couldn't get your daughter out of the country without a passport."

"Lucia has a passport," I said. "Back in May I sent the three of them out of the country for Lucia to be treated for torticollis in her neck. Jolie was not satisfied with treatment options here in the U.S. I agreed that if we ran out of options here then they could go abroad. Thankfully the treatment worked. So, yes, Lucia does have a passport. It just doesn't seem possible for Jolie to arrange a trip so quickly. It was only six days ago that we argued over custody."

Leaning closer to me, elbows resting on his knees, the officer said, "What do you mean?"

"Jolie and I recently agreed on divorce terms," I replied. "It should be pretty straight forward. But she said that she wanted to prolong the process and make it as expensive as possible for me. Then I said that I would do everything I could to get full custody of Lucia, which would eliminate our having to deal with one another."

In a softened tone the senior officer said, "Do you really think that could happen?"

"No," I mumbled, "it was said in the heat of the moment. Actually, I don't want anyone to be separated from Lucia."

The officer straightened his back and squared his shoulders. "Mr. Brown, right now there is nothing that we can do. A mother has the right to take her daughter until proven otherwise. So you must work through an attorney to get a judge to file an order designating full custody for your daughter to you. Once that order is in place your wife would be found in violation of the order, which would allow us to begin an investigation. But for now, unfortunately, we are unable to help you. I would suggest that if you hear from your wife you do your best to determine where she is because that could help with our investigation."

My voice blurted out of my throat, "I'm Lucia's father! Don't I have any rights? I'm telling you that my wife has basically stolen my daughter. I don't understand—this makes no sense at all. But you're telling me to wait for a judge to confirm it. If she hasn't already left the country processing a court order will certainly give her the time to do it!"

Standing up and keeping his gaze fixed on my face, the senior officer responded, "I understand your frustration. Unfortunately, there is nothing we can do for you at this time."

The two officers turned toward the door, and when I opened it for them I saw that the sun had set. This seemingly routine Saturday had evolved into an unbelievable, traumatic sequence. The weight of the events of the day settled in my feet and I could barely push them forward to cross the room. Tomorrow, Sunday, I would piece together the information from Jolie and help my family make arrangements for my aunt. Physical and emotional exhaustion took over and I slept.

At 9:00 a.m. on Sunday the first call that I made was to the attorney that I had consulted a few weeks ago about filing for divorce. I left a voicemail and an e-mail asking that he call me first thing on Monday.

Then I made an unsuccessful attempt to track Jolie through our cell phone GPS service. Since both of our phones are on the same account I reviewed her call logs for several days leading up to Saturday. It seemed strange but all phone activity ended on Thursday. The last five numbers dialed were all 800 numbers, and I dialed them all only to learn that they were banking and credit card customer service centers. Jolie did not have credit cards, her mother did, and perhaps she was inquiring about available lines of credit. It made sense that they would try to live off of credit cards for a while. However, none of that information pointed to where they could possibly have gone.

Next, I checked in with my parents and learned that arrangements for Aunt Varney's service had not been finalized and that out-of-town family members would soon be arriving.

On Monday morning I called my manager and left a voicemail advising that I needed to take the day off to handle a personal matter. Just seconds after 8:00 a.m. the attorney returned my call and agreed for me to come to his Philadelphia office at 10:00 a.m.

"David, I received both your e-mail and voicemail," he began. "The two of you had separated. Now it appears that your wife took your daughter, and you don't know where they are?"

"That's correct," I said.

"Do you have any idea why she would do this?" he countered.

My shoulders seemed to cave into my rib cage, and my eyes rolled up to the ceiling then down to the office floor. Before answering I struggled for a few seconds trying to lessen the nauseous sensation in my throat and twisting sensations in my stomach. I had been unable to eat for the past few days.

"It makes no sense to me," I whispered. "When I met with you a few weeks ago I explained that we were looking to divorce. Once my wife and I talked it through, we both seemed relieved and agreed to live separately, she with her mother, I in our apartment. Lucia was to spend weekends with me. Things were amicable. But last week, talking through details, Jolie questioned my request to file before the end of the year. I told her that I just wanted to move forward and offered that we could actually file the paperwork at the end of the year. I did, however, want us to agree on terms in advance of filing. Angrily, she countered by saying that she wanted it to be as expensive and painful as possible for me and that she would drag things out. Then I countered by saying that I would do everything I could to get full custody of Lucia. That was probably the trigger—it repeated in her e-mail."

Together we read through Saturday's e-mail from Jolie. Then the attorney said, "Pardon my bluntness. Was there any abuse in the household?"

"Absolutely not!" I said, raising my voice slightly. "Over the past few months we've raised our voices when we argued but that's about it. I guess that happens when couples are not getting along."

The attorney affirmed my statement with an up and down head nod while I inched my body forward to the edge of the chair. "So what are my options? I have no idea where Jolie and Lucia are. Communication stopped after Saturday's e-mail."

"First, we have to file a custody order with a judge, a process that takes about six weeks," he said. "At that point local law enforcement can begin trying to locate them."

The skin on my face burned like I had spiked a fever. "What do you mean it takes six weeks? That's entirely too long! No wonder people panic."

"We can always request an emergency custody order based on the circumstances. Since your wife is not a U.S. citizen we can argue that she is a flight risk," he replied.

"Yes, go ahead." I nodded. "So, what do we do next?"

The attorney leaned forward resting both elbows on his desk. "I will phone a professional contact in your county today who can probably meet with a judge fairly quickly. In the meantime, I require a retainer of $7,500 to cover initial services. And my rate is $350 per hour."

A soft gasp escaped from my throat on hearing the dollar figures. But I did not hesitate; Lucia was absolutely the most important person in my life. I felt that Jolie would always put Lucia's welfare first, yet immediate threats to her safety were unknown. Long term, I had deep concerns about Lucia's quality of life if my family and I were not actively involved. Although the attorney's experience in international abduction cases was limited, he provided initial information and referred me to the State Department website as well as the National Center for Missing and Exploited Children.

During the next few days confusion prevailed as I ran down clues on the whereabouts of my wife and daughter and delved into legal processes for parental abductions. My daughter was missing and my heart was overwhelmed with sadness, and at the same time I was utterly enraged that Jolie would have taken Lucia away. Though my family members, a few close friends, and my boss were aware I spent much of my time in complete isolation wanting to hide my anxiety, shame, and embarrassment from the rest of the world. My stomach felt knotted and constricted so I avoided eating. Close friends and family have always been supportive, but I feared hearing the proverbial, "I told you so." Hour after hour I backtracked phone records and replayed conversations in my head, hoping to uncover a clue to Jolie's whereabouts. I phoned all of her friends that I knew, including Carla who was still local. All of them appeared to be as stunned as I. Initially, I didn't believe Carla when she told me that she had not heard from Jolie. It seemed too farfetched that she could have completely vanished without any indication to anyone. Or did the suddenness of Jolie's actions indicate the magnitude of her concerns and fears?

Thinking that focusing on something else might ease the pain, on the fourth day I went to the office and tried to work a full eight hours, only to find that it was impossible. Fragments of momentary calm that I had achieved were completely undone any time coworkers and unaware friends casually asked about my weekend or Lucia or Jolie. As a professional I had learned early in my career that maintaining composure was key to being perceived as managing and controlling situations. Yet the physical and emotional pain was tearing me apart inside, and I simply could not manage. Nor was I ready to talk about it broadly, especially not knowing where Jolie and Lucia were. I was surprised and appreciative that confidentiality was maintained by the few people whom I had told directly what had happened. My family was still grieving the loss of my aunt, so I decided to take some additional days to be with them and to try to manage worry and fear for my daughter.

Five days passed with no communication or signs of my wife and daughter. On the sixth morning, I received the signed custody order from my attorney and immediately took it to the local police. The order granted me full custodial rights to Lucia until a hearing could be held mid-December. Once I presented the custody order to the local authorities they took action and re-interviewed me about the circumstances of Lucia's abduction as well as initiated a search of the local neighborhood. The aching tension in my body reduced slightly, and I breathed a little easier knowing that my situation had been taken seriously. I was instructed to go home and wait for one of the officers to call me with next steps.

Three anxious hours passed then my phone rang. "Hello, this is David," I said.

A stern male voice responded, "Mr. Brown, this is Officer Howard. You and I spoke a few hours ago down at the police station."

I raised the volume in my voice to match his. "Yes, Officer Howard, do you have any news?"

There was a pause and I could hear the phone receiver shuffling in his hand. "Mr. Brown, are you sitting down?"

I quickly replied, "Yes!" Then I heard Officer Howard's deep inhale.

"I hate to tell you, but we have been able to confirm that your wife, daughter, and mother-in-law were listed on the passenger list of a plane routed from JFK to Uzbekistan. They left the United States last Thursday."

"What?!" I said in disbelief.

"I'm very sorry, Mr. Brown," he replied.

I pulled myself together momentarily and said, "What do I do now?"

Officer Howard responded, "I suggest contacting the State Department for guidance. They usually handle these types of situations. Someone there can explain the process for attempting to get your daughter back."

I sighed and could only muster up a muffled, "Thank you for your help."

Disconnecting the call, I slumped into the couch touching shoulders, spine, and neck into the cushions. "I'm a good person, and I truly love my daughter," I whispered to the empty room. "Why would something like this happen to me?"

Questions raced around my mind. How was I going to get Lucia back? Could Jolie have thought things were bad enough to leave the country without any warning? What am I supposed to do now? Not even a fragment of an answer came to me. Then the cell phone sitting on my lap vibrated before the ringtone startled me. Caller ID confirmed it was my sister. My emotions were very raw, so I tried to control my voice and tentatively said, "Hello."

"I am checking to see how you're doing today," my sister said.

It only took hearing her voice and all of the body muscles I had been clinching let go releasing a sob, followed by more sobs. "Jolie took Lucia to Uzbekistan!" My sister's reply was inaudible as wave after wave of emotion and tension spilled out.

More than a minute passed before my sister's voice faded back in, "Dee Jay, try to breathe. It's going to be okay. You will get through this." She heard me gasp for breath, cough out the catch in my throat, and inhale deeply. "That's better. Take in big breaths, deeper just like that," she soothed.

Once my breaths steadied I spoke again, "We exchanged text messages on Wednesday. Ten minutes ago the local police confirmed that Jolie, her mom, and Lucia were on a flight to Uzbekistan. They left Thursday. So she either couldn't receive messages from me on Friday—or chose to ignore them."

Softly my sister prodded, "So do you know where they could be or what your next steps are?"

The sound of my own voice was unfamiliar and quavering as I responded, "I don't know. I just don't know. Let me call you back in a little while." I disconnected the call, straightened my back against the couch frame, closed my eyes, and applied all of my inner resources to calm and clear my thoughts for the next fifteen minutes.

The Acceptance Principle

Practicing the principle of acceptance does not mean throwing up your hands or resigning. Instead, it means to calmly stop protesting what has already occurred and the surrounding circumstances. Whatever has happened in the immediate or distant past is unchangeable by you in this present moment. Although it might be possible to re-aggravate feelings, or even soften or smooth them, nonetheless the event is permanently located in yesterday, last month, or years ago in a time that has already passed. By stretching out to reach for acceptance you are on the way to reconnecting with your higher self and calmness.

Five days lapsed between receiving that frightening e-mail and law enforcement's confirmation that Jolie, Lucia, and Ami's names appeared on the manifest of a flight to Uzbekistan. I walked around in a haze, feeling like I was an unwilling character in a surreal movie. Hour after hour I debated with myself and attempted to form logical statements as to Jolie's motivations for leaving the country with Lucia. I put so much energy into asking and answering impossible questions that I began to lose traction with all other aspects of life—finding my daughter, comforting my family, maintaining my job, etc. Feeling incredibly scattered, it was very difficult to even see myself as someone who routinely handles situations and gets things resolved. Then I came to the intersection of denial and acceptance.

In that moment, when I brought to a complete halt the debates and protests going inside my mind and accepted that I had zero control over what had already happened, an amazing source of strength swept over me. I had never experienced anything like it, and the power of it pushed me right out of the seat of "victim."

Compassionate feelings began to expand for Jolie and Lucia and stretched out to everything and everyone around me. Positive, helpful sensations came back to me many times over, until I realized that like attracts like. In other words, what I send out into my environment is what I receive from it. Within a month relationships and the energy around me were incredibly improved because I was generating understanding and collaboration. Conversations with local law enforcement, the FBI, the National Center for Missing and Exploited Children, and the State Department had initially been marred by my anxiety to instantly reunite with my daughter. My family, friends, and coworkers support was expanded and bolstered by this new accepting and allowing version of me. I found myself in an emotionally safe and protected place. I nurtured a belief that as profoundly negative as it was for Jolie to leave with Lucia, there was an equal possibility of profound joy occurring. So why would I ever want to create or perpetuate limiting thoughts and beliefs? The desire to shift from resistance to acceptance completely took over, and I moved forward into openness, having formed a new space in my heart for acceptance, infinite possibilities, and renewable strength.

The following reflection questions are related to
the Acceptance Principle:

R Are you aware of time that you spend asking and
answering impossible questions? How does it affect your
E energy levels?

F Is there an event that has happened in your life that
would offer relief to you if you put it into a place of
L acceptance right now?

E

C How often and in what ways have you found yourself
trying to control the outcomes of the environment
T around you?

I

O Do you attempt to control the people around you rather
than allowing them the freedom to choose? How is your
N relationship with these individuals impacted?

S

Before reading this principle did you feel positive or
negative about the idea of "surrendering"?

CHAPTER 5:
THE COMPASSION PRINCIPLE

It is not always easy to imagine how
someone else is feeling or their motivations,
especially when they are suffering or lash out.

Dear Lucia,

We have many muscles in our wonderful bodies that easily bend and stretch and help us move. When you are playing, your muscles are really busy. Think of your heart as your special "compassion muscle." Compassion is fueled by our feelings, and applying compassion is one of the most powerful life principles. When we experience tender feelings of sympathy, sorrow, or empathy for others we are demonstrating compassion. It is not always easy to imagine how someone else is feeling or their motivations, especially when they are suffering or lash out at us. By choosing to live compassionately, your understanding and discernment will deepen and broaden. Seeing others through compassionate eyes is a form of humane, universal love. When you intend well-being for others and hold them in your heart, you are radiating a positive energy to all with whom you interact: people, animals, nature, and the whole environment. Every time you send compassionate love out to others it comes back to you in greater and greater quantities, and you will also enjoy a wonderful sense of freedom.

I love you, my dear,

Daddy

For several weeks after Lucia's abduction I battled gyrating emotions. Day-to-day responsibilities and activities served as numbing distractions to keep me moving forward. Otherwise I would have confined myself to a dark room to hide my grief and embarrassment from the world. I was so angry with Jolie and felt that she had betrayed my trust in the worst way. In a mere thirty-six hours my daughter had been taken away, and the loss and love for her evoked a piercing, unimaginable pain. Repeatedly, I pushed my emotions down, hiding them in a solitary place, an abyss that I dreaded having to face.

Everyone around me was empathetic and supportive, still I tried my best to compartmentalize so that my emotions weren't a distraction at work or overriding in personal relationships. It was important to me to appear to be grounded and functioning even while dealing with these traumatic circumstances. Discernable to me, but not evident to others, was the sensation of a bulky weight in the pit of my stomach, like a thousand-pound ship anchor. Although the emotional anchor didn't protrude from my body, or clank when I walked, I sensed its presence in the undulating emotions scrolling from my abdomen to diaphragm to ribs to heart to throat, up and down, up and down. When the swell reached my heart I often broke down and cried, triggered by the end of a day when my small energy reserve was depleted from answering well-meaning inquiries. I attempted to deal directly with questions because seeing friends, family, and coworkers tip-toe around me increased my anxiety. Their faces and body language shouted discomfort and awkwardness while their hearts were full of sympathy and concern for my well-being. My emotionless mask probably contributed to their discomfort.

The Sunday before Thanksgiving marked three weeks since Jolie had left with Lucia. Just moments before opening my eyes I was floating on the edge of a lovely dream. Waking to feelings of anxiety had become routine, and during the day waves of feeling overwhelmed repeated hour to hour. But this early morning dream held images of Lucia walking toward me, and it felt so real that my breathing quickened and colors intensified ten times brighter. Lucia's dark-brown hair had grown down to her shoulders, much longer than the last time I saw her. She wore a pretty white dress with ruffles and lace and small, white patent leather shoes. The image was angelic, radiating with so much love. Her smile broadened with every step, and my excitement grew as she came closer and closer. When I knelt down to greet her she jumped onto my lap, wrapping her little arms around my neck. I drew closer, leaning forward so that our faces almost touched, and she kissed me on the cheek. "Everything is going to be okay, Daddy," she whispered in my right ear. I felt her small breaths gently gracing my face as she spoke. In that sweet moment I was filled with a profound sense of peace, and it cascaded over me like a spring shower. This sense of peace soaked through me, permeating my senses head to toe. The dream seemed both long and short—then I woke up.

Was it a fleeting dream or a vibrational connection that Lucia had made with me? For the next fifteen minutes I lay as still as possible, slowing my breathing, squeezing out of my body and memory every drop of detail of Lucia in imagery, words, and feelings. Missing her so much, my impulse was to pour harsh logic on the experience, but thankfully, the beautiful, peaceful feelings prevailed. It was like taking the best parts of the best dream you ever had and shifting them into conscious awareness.

I spent most of the remainder of that day at the apartment cleaning up and organizing information and notes from multiple conversations with various law enforcement officials, government agencies, and my attorney. Throughout the morning images of Lucia popped up everywhere. My intuition was on high alert, and I believed that it all meant something very significant. And the more times I thought about Lucia, the better I felt and the more peace I experienced. Around 11:00 a.m. I began my daily meditation.

Over the past three years, after an inspiring conversation with a friend and reading a few online articles about its benefits, I began to reserve time every day for meditation. Through my early discovery I found Zen meditation to be the practice that I most enjoyed. Daily meditation time has become central to my overall mental and spiritual well-being. Pushing away distractions, being very present, and beginning with a focus on rhythmic breathing has become my primary process for grounding and self-awareness. I am always refreshed after setting aside all distractions and experiencing fifteen to twenty minutes in complete silence. Beginning with gentle, purposeful breathing I am gradually able to release chaotic thoughts and ease into calmness. Some days the meditations went far deeper. Over time, I learned not to judge outcomes and experienced increased gratitude for honoring this practice.

On this day, in readiness for meditation, I positioned myself in the corner of the "L" of the large sectional sofa, an old friend by now. A lot of natural light streams through the sliding glass door behind the couch, and the texture of the upholstery is very comfortable. So I sat cross-legged in the couch corner, positioning a bright-red pillow under one knee, and a multicolored one on the other side. Adding the pillows eliminated the potential for cramping provoked by an old hip injury. My iPad sat on the adjacent dark-brown, circular, wooden coffee table, and I picked it up to select meditation music that featured Tibetan chimes or nature sounds, which deeply resonated with me. I found a music video of a forest and meandering path that opened onto a private beach. The gentle rhythms invited me to focus on my breathing and gradually relax.

I began with deep inhales from my diaphragm followed by controlled exhales that activated expansion/retraction of my stomach. The flurry of daily-life thoughts and worries gradually dissipated with each cycle of breaths. As my mental chatter subsided, the music of the soft chimes took over, accompanied by the nature sounds of crashing waves and chirping birds. After a few moments I also heard drops of rain gently falling on tree leaves. It was a symphony of nature with many textures enhanced by my own mental images. In a few minutes, by focusing on my breathing, random thoughts stopped, and I was completely present, just being.

The early morning dream of Lucia returned, however, this time I was an observer watching her talk to me as she sat on my lap. All too soon her image faded and the scene changed to a crowded airport terminal. Many men and women in business suits and professional attire hustled to their respective gates. Then the organized chaos began to divide, and three beings emerged from the distance. Although everything around them was hazy, I experienced a laser-like focus to their silhouettes and the shifting light around them. From left to right, they stood in stair-step heights. A bag strap draped over the left shoulder of the tallest person while the left hand rolled a suitcase. The middle person's left hand guided a wheeled suitcase while the right hand gripped the outstretched hand of the smallest being. The trio's walking pace slowed as they drew closer to me. Frame by frame I anticipated identifying individual faces. The fog cleared and revealed Jolie, her mom, and Lucia. In the instant that Lucia and I made eye contact and smiled at each other she released Jolie's hand and toddled toward me. We hugged. I kissed her cheeks and my tears flowed as I buried my face into her small shoulder. Sobbing and trying to speak I stood to address Jolie and her mother. I brushed tears away with the back of my hand, and my words jumbled as I began to thank them for coming back. Neither woman spoke a word but stared at me expressionless. Before I could say more the vision ended and the trio vanished. Streaming through the patio door the pre-winter sun warmed the back of my neck, and I returned to consciousness.

What felt like a mere ten minutes had actually been forty-five minutes of deep meditation. As I stretched arms and legs, releasing my meditation posture, a discernable flow of calmness and ease moved through me. Much of the negativity I felt about circumstances and my anger toward Jolie about Lucia's abduction was beginning to reduce. The words I heard Lucia speak in last night's dream warmed my heart and comforted me, and today's vision of our reunion ignited a flame of hope that I would soon see my daughter.

The following day, November 25th, was Lucia's first birthday. I didn't know what to expect emotionally, however, I was committed to celebrating her first year of life, even if it was by myself. I told my family about celebrating Lucia's special day although we would not be together. My plan was to have a quiet, honorary moment by myself. That morning, before heading out the door to work, I grabbed a small white box from the refrigerator and carefully walked down the stairs to the car. I popped the trunk open, placing laptop and lunch inside, however, the white box was so special that it would ride in the front seat beside me.

Normally, I enter the office exchanging pleasantries with anyone who makes eye contact, and today was the same. The frequency of inquiries from my colleagues had died down a bit. They all perceived that trying to locate Jolie and Lucia would be a lengthy process. So my personal situation was no longer a topic of conversation at the water cooler. Before going to my desk, I stopped by our common area, which is like a break room on steroids: 10,000 square feet of open space and seating, four refrigerators, six microwaves, and multiple coffee/tea stations. I positioned my lunch bag on the top shelf of an uncrowded refrigerator, pushing it toward a back corner hoping that any would-be lunch thieves would believe the food content was old.

Laptop bag strap positioned on my left shoulder, I carefully carried the small white box with two hands and exited the common area. Reaching my desk, I placed the box in the corner somewhat out of sight and began daily routines by booting up my computer. The morning passed slowly with no office brush fires to put out, and my teams ran productively, requiring minimal input from me. As the noon hour approached I decided to retrieve my lunch bag from the refrigerator and eat at my desk, thereby skirting well-meaning questions or the distractions of the large common area. I slid the white box directly in front of me and slowly traced the lettering on the box with my right index finger, Felix's Caketeria. Jolie had discovered this little gem of an establishment in an adjacent town. Our shared love for sweets made Felix's a favorite place to treat ourselves now and then. Inside the box was a beautiful yellow cupcake topped with white buttercream fondant icing plus red, white, blue, and yellow streamers and small pieces of sugar confetti. Had Lucia been here in person there would have been a box full of Felix's cupcakes for her birthday. I offered a silent prayer to the benevolent universe earnestly hoping for the return of my daughter and a positive resolution to current circumstances. Then, before taking a bite, I snapped a picture of the pretty cupcake and sent a hopeful e-mail to Jolie asking that she give Lucia a big hug and birthday kiss from me. The cupcake was as delicious as any I have ever eaten from Felix's, made even sweeter by the symbolism of the moment and that my tension-filled emotions were continuing to lift.

Over the next three days my positive emotions continued to slowly rise, fueled by increasingly powerful meditations. The rushing flow of negative emotions that had held my stomach hostage began to dissipate, and my appetite returned. Thinking processes were becoming clearer, and my awareness of these changes sparked even more eagerness for this continuing evolution. More and more the hazy feeling was lifting, and my heart seemed to be expanding, encouraged by the words that Lucia spoke in the dream, "Everything is going to be okay, Daddy." Intuitively I knew that no matter what happened, everything was going to work out. The clarity that I was now experiencing urged me toward an empathetic understanding of Jolie's motivations. When I was overflowing with negative emotions, feelings of anger and betrayal ruled, however, as those harsh feelings subsided, I was able to emotionally remove myself from the bare circumstances and view Jolie's decision judgment free. Although I could not replicate her exact feelings, it became abundantly clear to me that she was operating out of fear and that false evidence appeared real to her. In her e-mail announcing that she had taken Lucia out of the country, Jolie wrote that she feared losing custody of Lucia. Now, gazing through a peaceful calm and clarity, I reflected on our circumstances. I realized an unprecedented compassion and profound discovery.

If Jolie had made this decision out of fear, where did it come from? Up to this point in time we had agreed on everything related to getting a divorce. For both of us there seemed to be a sense of relief about going our separate ways, dissolving the marriage, and maintaining joint custody of Lucia. On November 3rd we argued about the timing of filing for divorce, and during our heated exchange she warned that she would do her best to draw the process out and drive up divorce expenses. I countered and said that I would bypass her and seek full custody of Lucia. Had that statement initiated Jolie's fear and triggered this agonizing situation? In the middle of an argument when compassion and sympathy may be quashed, people often say things they don't truly mean. My pronouncement to seek full custody of Lucia was an idle threat, so I assumed Jolie's threats were also empty. But were they?

Self-blame coursed through me, but the newly found inner

peace held back loathing thoughts. Focusing and contemplating, I tried to put myself in Jolie's shoes and worked to imagine her core emotions. Using my newly found feelings of empathy, I practiced articulating her decision saying it out loud, moving her rationale around in my mind. Over and over I touched emotions and feelings that could have been moving through Jolie, and gradually an unblocking of my understanding began. In this unfamiliar place, the knots of anger entangling my heart released, and I felt compassion and awareness growing in all directions. It was all completely new to me. After months of anguish in what seemed like a burst of lightening I understood that the decision Jolie had made had been significantly impacted by a convergence of inconsistent and jagged edges of her total life experience up to that point. Prior to falling in love and coming together, our life situations had been extremely different, making it almost impossible for me to fully understand her decision-making rationale. Many diverse factors must have influenced Jolie's conclusions. Even so, I knew in my heart and full capacity that the fear she was running from was nonexistent. I began to experience a profound sense of compassion towards Jolie.

All of us have had times when we were fearful, which impacted the shape and definition of our individual perceptions. Now in my new empathetic understanding, I have been able to recognize ways in which many of my actions contributed to Jolie's uncertainty and fearfulness. But I can't place total blame on myself or accept accountability for her actions. We are only able to be accountable for our own actions, not the actions of others. We are in control of our own choice making, and we always have choices to make about how we will react, respond, or not respond to actions that others take.

Here is a stirring question: Would you or I prefer to live proactively or reactively?

The retaliatory comment I made during our argument may have sparked fear within Jolie. At that time she was a full-time student finishing her four-year degree, and I was a U.S. citizen with a full-time job. I will never be able to speak for her or be inside her feelings at that pivotal moment. In her mind it may have seemed that things were stacked against her. For many days afterward those thoughts circulated in my heart and mind as I realized that the fear she experienced was quite possibly beyond anything I could have ever imagined.

Words—words—blurted out in an emotional moment, insignificant to me five minutes later, had for Jolie morphed into a tangible threat. And from her perspective the potential for losing custody of Lucia was so real and urgent that she took immediate, radical action. Just four days after our argument, Jolie left the country taking our daughter with her.

This Thanksgiving was especially emotional for my entire family for several reasons. It was the first time that we had all been together since my aunt's passing. Thanksgiving has always been my favorite holiday, but this year neither my daughter nor wife was here. The previous Thanksgiving we were eager for Lucia to be born, and our excitement and anticipation made the holiday even more special. This year I was somewhat withdrawn, standing away from the group, staring out windows. Not given to openly expressing a lot of emotion, my family's laughter and good-natured kidding were very comforting throughout the day. It might have been easier if I had been angry and challenged being thankful when so much was missing. But I was unwilling to allow anger to rule and risk suppressing my expanding shift in perspective.

Like peeling an onion layer by layer, deeper reflections revealed new truths. What had been profound disbelief grew into a steady stream of awareness about labeling myself as a victim. I "got it." Now I perceived myself as the opposite of victim. With new eyes I looked beyond immediate circumstances and began seeing repeating patterns in news reports, articles, and defenses of daily behaviors. I asked myself, "What tiny portion do we really see or understand of one another?"

Many of us exert minimal efforts to understand others because we are engrossed in finding our own way and hampered by the personal baggage that we drag along. Occasionally, we try to put ourselves in another person's space not realizing that "today" is only a snapshot of myriad experiences that underpin any individual's moment-to-moment decisions. Many of us classify things and/or events as "good" or "bad" based on how we anticipate outcomes. And the anticipated outcome is based solely on perceptions of our immediate world and momentary vantage points. When the other person's decision making does not align with our own beliefs or logic, we are prone to judge it and them negatively. In my case, being disconnected from Jolie's perspective, and responding from my singular, angry vantage point, translated into fear and upheaval for multiple lives.

I have always felt that Jolie's desire was to put Lucia first, the ultimate sacrifice for any parent. It is a strong position, and I truly commend her for it. For many months I have asked myself, "How much of our situation is about Jolie and me, rather than what is best for Lucia?" Today, feeling the flow of compassion and experiencing new awareness, those angry thoughts are gone, blown away like leaves and twigs disbursed by yesterday's rain storm.

The Compassion Principle

Experiencing two huge, traumatic events in one day—my aunt's passing and Lucia's abduction—was so overwhelming that my only accessible responses were anxiety, anger, upset, embarrassment, resentment, and shame. Feelings of compassion, pity, or mercy for Jolie seemed as far away as the moon. But when Lucia appeared in my dream saying that everything would be okay, I was the recipient of mercy followed by peaceful understanding. It was the pivotal step in my personal awakening, and I began to see everything and everyone with new eyes.

Of course there were low days and painful nights when I cried myself to sleep, anxious about my baby girl, wishing to sing to her and watch her take her first steps. Yet most prominent within my new understanding was that my very significant emotions and feelings were as real as Jolie's quest to be unrestricted and fear of losing Lucia. So I can't judge, nor can I define, the impact on Lucia when at eleven months old she suddenly stopped being with her daddy. As she grows and evolves so will her views of herself, her mother, and her father. It is my deepest desire that the heartbreak that the three of us have felt will evolve into heart openings, expanding our empathy, compassion, and sensitivity toward others.

Life is dynamic and ever changing, and for me, that is really inviting. However, some people get stuck or become trapped in suffering, discomfort, and unhappiness. I was able to receive the compassion and mercy that was already there because my angry guard was down. When we are engaged in activities that distract us from negative, anxious thoughts, such as resting, sleeping, or meditating, our protests and resistances stop and the floodgates open for the comfort and compassion that was ours all along.

This crisis that launched my personal awakening has continued to reveal more and more opportunities to practice loving-kindness, compassion, and empathetic understanding. Going about my daily life, and certainly in meditation, I began to hold all of us in a place of compassion. In a short period of time this compassionate space has become my heart center for Lucia, Jolie, friends, family, coworkers, myself, and expanding out to the wider world. I have never felt anything so good!

The following reflection questions are related to
the Compassion Principle:

R **E**	Have you been paying attention to your dreams? What are two messages you have recently received?
F **L**	How does it feel in your heart when you hold a space of compassion for another person?
E **C** **T**	How does it feel when you receive compassion from another person?
I **O**	Have you experienced a heart renovation? What changed? What is continuing?
N **S**	If you were going to honor someone else's situation today, who would it be and why?

CHAPTER 6:
THE FORGIVENESS PRINCIPLE

Remember to forgive yourself, and the rest is up to
the other person and out of your control.

Dear Lucia,

It is wonderful when we are able to enjoy happy interactions with many different people that we know and don't know. Yet there may be other times when situations are harsh and things are said or done that are hurtful. My hope for you is that when you feel hurt or disappointed that you will truly want to stand back from the situation, become an observer, and endeavor to understand the other person's feelings or experience. You are expressing empathy when you use your power of understanding to imagine how another person is feeling and responding. Each time you tap into that awareness, you will move much closer to practicing forgiveness and acceptance.

However, when emotions are painful and prolonged it creates a strain as heavy and awkward as it would be for one single person to pull a giant tractor-trailer. Everyone involved feels the discomfort. Sometimes suppressed negative emotions can become an unpleasant surprise when they bounce into an unrelated situation seeming to show up out of nowhere! It may not be the easiest thing to do, but the sense of freedom that you will derive from a few minutes of envisioning yourself in the other person's place will be very empowering. You can't force anyone to accept the forgiveness that you offer to them. Remember to love and forgive yourself, and the rest is up to the other person and out of your control. If you will make it your intention to respect the other person's right to have and express their feelings and hold them in a space of compassion, you will be sharing loving-kindness and also caring for yourself. When forgiveness flows right from your heart the other person will sense it and, hopefully, move on to a place of better feelings. My dear one, you are learning all the time and are magnificent! Always remember that.

I love you,

Daddy

Thirty days after Jolie left the country I felt submerged by the crisis and sporadic anger toward her. Both mentally and physically I felt exhausted from trying to maintain professional balance, figure out next steps for tracking Jolie's whereabouts, and preparing to temporarily move back in with my parents. On Friday evening after a long and busy workweek, I stopped by a favorite Chinese takeout located around the corner from our apartment. Jolie and I had a routine of getting takeout on Friday nights, and so far, I did not have the heart to stop the pattern. Our order was always the same: General Tso's chicken, fried rice, and steamed dumplings. It was more than enough for both of our suppers and allowed for tasty leftovers for the next day.

Arriving home I placed the containers of supper on the counter and opened a bottle of Sauvignon Blanc to enjoy with my meal. The first sip brought a welcome wave of decompression, and I closed my eyes expecting to taste citrus and melon in the New Zealand wine. Ready to enjoy the meal, I placed two dumplings, a portion of General Tso's chicken, and some fried rice on my plate then sat solo at the table. It might have been the first moment of true relaxation of the entire week.

After eating dinner, even though I was exhausted, I aimlessly watched several movies. With no commitments for Saturday I granted myself the privilege of making this a stress-free evening. At my usual 11:00 p.m. bedtime I slid between the sheets and very quickly sank into a deep slumber.

When the moonlight was still peering through the bedroom blinds, my eyes popped open. Stretching my arms out and yawning, I spoke to the empty room, "What time is it?" Then I grabbed my phone from the dresser and saw 3:15 a.m. displayed on the screen. Silently conversing with myself, I wondered, "What in the world am I doing up? And why do I feel so alert after being exhausted only a few hours ago?"

Sleeping was my goal, so I put the phone down and adjusted the bed covers. A few minutes passed and I realized that my overloaded mind was fixated on Jolie and Lucia. Maybe pulsing questions had woken me up, and now I felt compelled to untangle inner thoughts and feelings. Several weeks had passed since I had dreamed of Lucia when she had told me everything would be okay. In these early morning hours that little taste of peace was being dismissed by a new sense of urgency. Then a flash of insight hit me, and I knew the next step to take to reach more calm and peace. I reached for my phone, sat upright, and leaned against the headboard and began keying in a message.

> *Jolie,*
>
> *As I'm sure you can imagine, the last month has been the most difficult of my life. My heart breaks because Lucia is not here. Also, on the day that I received your e-mail, my aunt passed away. So my family has been trying to cope with both of these tragedies. And it hasn't been easy.*
>
> *For me personally, what has been interesting is the series of emotions that have shown up over the past month. My friends, family, and coworkers expect me to be angry and revengeful. For me, this time has been quite the opposite. What has flowed from my broken heart is such an overwhelming sense of peace and compassion. Let me explain. You and I have had a rough few months leading up to this. And though I would never want to separate either of us from Lucia, I believe the time apart is really needed for us to heal. You've never liked when I've been apologetic, so I won't use this as a forum to do that. However, understand that I accept my part in this entire situation that has led you to have such a great sense of fear that you believed that I would want to separate you from Lucia.*

With no pauses or hesitation words surged from my heart into my fingers so fast that it was a challenge to keep up. I typed as fast as I could to reach the crux of what I wanted to share with Jolie.

> *And with that comes compassion. I am compassionate because you don't have to feel the way that you do. Though we didn't always get along, and we were going our separate ways, my family and I would ensure that you and Lucia would never have to do without the things you need. And yes, we might disagree at times*

*as to what that looks like, but there would always be
support. That is why I always asked about your plan.
With the time that has passed, I have reached a point
of clarity. And I want you to know two things that I
hope resonate with you. The first thing that I want
you to know is that I forgive you. I don't think anyone
can truly understand the pain that I feel every single
day. But, despite that, I, without question, forgive you.
The second thing that I want you to understand is that
when you are ready to come back to the U.S., I will do
whatever I have to in order to help you and Lucia get
here and get on your feet. The current circumstances
are really a lose-lose for everyone. You have given up
your academic career and the goals you had, Lucia is
without the balance of having her father around, and
my side of the family doesn't get to see the growth of
their granddaughter, niece, etc. Someone that I know
asks about Lucia every single day. That is a form of
love that she may never experience. My hope is that
one day you have a moment of clarity to where you see
this situation similar to me. But, more importantly, I
hope that you understand that there are options that
can work for everyone. And hopefully that will lead you
to also finding peace and compassion.*

*Be well,
David*

When the words and emotions stopped streaming through, and even without proof-reading, I automatically hit "send." It was hugely important to me for this heartfelt message to go to Jolie and that she would read that my battle armor had been removed and that I genuinely wanted to be in Lucia's life and help her as long as I could. I let out a deep and peaceful sigh as my outpouring of sincerity and compassion filled every part of me.

With my phone inches away from my face, I lay back down hoping in every way that Jolie would respond right away and tell me that she wanted to come home. For the next hour I watched

and waited, constantly refreshing e-mails willing a reply from
Jolie to come. Finally, I laid the phone in the empty space next
to me on the bed and slept.

It seemed like only minutes before the sun rose. I waited
until about 8:30 a.m. to get out of bed to begin some light
cleaning and packing for the move back to my parents' house in
three weeks. Around noon I left the apartment and walked the
short distance to the property manager's office to confirm timing
and logistics for my upcoming move out of the apartment.
Meredith, the property manager, a middle-aged Caucasian
woman, and I had met a week ago when I asked to get out of
my lease. She was very understanding and agreed to return my
security deposit and that there would be no penalty. Though
we had only spoken twice, once on the phone and once face to
face, each time it was difficult to keep my voice from quavering
and my eyes dry. The process of moving out of the apartment
made even more prominent the fact that I was not able to be
with Lucia and of what I considered to be a personal failure.
Her sense of compassion and kindness was very evident as she
always shared encouraging words, and I was incredibly grateful
for her sincerity and level of accommodation.

As I entered the leasing office, Meredith and her assistant
were standing next to a work table, and they immediately
greeted me in unison, "Hi, David!"

I smiled back at them and said, "Hello, ladies!"

"How can I help you today, David?" Meredith began. "And
how are preparations for your move going?"

I rested one hand on the top edge of the chair pushed
against Meredith's desk and replied, "It's going well. I do have
a question. When can I go into Ami's apartment and look for
anything of Lucia's that I can keep?"

Meredith answered, "I will call the maintenance person on
duty and ask him to let you in right now if you have time."

"That would be great, Meredith," I acknowledged. "Should
I go there now?"

Meredith nodded and picked up the phone to call
maintenance. I thanked her for her time and made my way to the
exit. As I gripped the knob and opened the door I turned back to
Meredith and said, "I want to thank you again for being so kind

and understanding during this time. I know that you don't have to do any of the things you are doing for me. They mean so much to me and my family."

Her eyes welled with tears that spilled onto her lashes. "Thank you, David. If there is anything I can do to continue helping you, please let me know. I wish you all the best and will continue to pray for you and your family."

Her compassionate response triggered even more emotion from me and haltingly I spoke one more time, "Thank you, Meredith. That means a lot to me."

Ami's third-floor apartment was two buildings away from the leasing office, and I covered the distance and flights of stairs before the maintenance man's arrival. Moments later a lanky, twenty-something male with scruffy facial hair nodded to me as he walked up the stairs to unlock the apartment door. After unlocking the door and staying less than a minute, he headed back down the stairs calling to me over his shoulder, "Lock up when you are done."

The apartment was just as I remembered from thirty days ago. The furniture was still in place and bags of clothing and trash dotted the area. I absorbed the energy in the room, feeling much less frantic and anxious than before. There used to be so much love here between all of us and the tender caring for Lucia. Today this final visit to Ami's abandoned apartment was calmer, almost comforting, influenced by the release that I felt from the pre-dawn e-mail that I had written to Jolie. Slowly I searched drawers and bags finding one item to keep, the wooden high chair purchased for Lucia a few months ago. In all of this disarray its newness stood out to me. Standing there, rubbing the back of the high chair, images passed through my mind, and I recalled feeding dinner to Lucia as she sat in this pretty chair the last time I was with her. The high chair was especially sentimental to me because it was one of the few larger purchases that I personally selected for Lucia. Most of Lucia's other furniture was either selected by Jolie or was a gift.

After picking up the chair and plastic booster seat I walked to the doorway and scanned the apartment one more time. Then I flipped the lock and closed the door behind me. After the short walk back to my apartment I went to the bedroom where Lucia slept when she stayed with me and put the high chair next to a packing box that I had labeled for her toys and crib accessories. Even though my emotions were still raw, this morning's events revealed the soft edges of a sense of ease about the next transition and a calming that was comforting. I was eager to extend it with today's meditation, and I walked to the couch and settled into the familiar corner to focus on my breathing.

The Forgiveness Principle

Accepting or rejecting forgiveness cannot be forced. However, earnestly expressing empathy and forgiveness is potentially more significant to the sender than to the receiver. Acting authentically initiates a cleansing effect for the sender as well as for the shared energy of both parties. If I had not worked to release my pain and jagged feelings, I would have cemented myself to them and disabled any forward movement. Transition into the next part of my journey would have stalled out.

Remnants of the dream when Lucia whispered to me, "Everything's going to be okay, Daddy," returned many times, and each time I was comforted and infused with peaceful feelings. Even so, a subtle uneasiness was still there and may well have been what woke me at 3:15 a.m. and led me to write to Jolie and express my feelings of compassion. At my core I realized that long-lasting inner peace wasn't achievable until I had released my anxiety and anger toward Jolie.

To this day I have not received a response from my early morning e-mail. Several times I have reread the original e-mail that I sent and wished that I had emphasized empathy. Forgiveness and empathy are equally important, and my understanding and energy are very different now. The original e-mail, though heartfelt, could be interpreted as carrying a slight tone of judgment. It might have come across as, "If you comply with what I want and make me happy, I will do 'X' for you." On the morning that I wrote the initial e-mail, and even more so today, I truly want Jolie to understand that I was sincerely trying to express empathy by feeling what she was feeling. If I were to send that e-mail today, here is what I would say...

Jolie,

As I'm sure you can imagine the last month has been the most difficult of my life. My heart breaks over and over because Lucia is not here. Also, my aunt passed away on the same day that I received your e-mail about leaving with Lucia. My family and I have been trying to cope with both of these tragedies. It has all been very painful.

Over the past month my emotions have been on a roller coaster. My friends, family, and coworkers have expected me to be angry and revengeful. But I have felt quite the opposite. Flowing through my broken heart is an overwhelming sense of compassion. You and I have had a rough few months leading up to this. And though I would never want either of us to be separated from Lucia, I believe the time apart will lead to healing. Since you have never liked when I've been apologetic, I won't use this as a forum to do that. However, please know that I accept my part in this situation that evoked such a great sense of fear that you believed that I wanted to separate you from Lucia.

I am filled with compassion and want you to know that you do not have to be fearful. Even though we didn't always get along, and had agreed to divorce, my family and I would ensure that you and Lucia would never have to do without the things you need. And yes, we might disagree about the specifics at times, but support would always be there. During these difficult days I have experienced points of clarity. And I want you to know two important things that I hope will resonate with you. I don't think anyone can truly understand the emptiness and daily pain that I feel, but regardless, and without question, I am empathetic to your feelings and offer forgiveness to you. The second thing that I want you to know is that when you are ready to come back to the U.S., I will do all that I can to help you and Lucia get here and get on your feet. The current circumstances benefit no one, least of all Lucia. I am sad that you have given up your academic studies and your career goals, that Lucia is missing her father, and that my family is unable to enjoy watching their granddaughter grow. Every day someone close to me asks about Lucia, and she is missing that form of love. My deep and sincere hope is that one day you will experience a clarity that will allow you to perceive this situation from both of our viewpoints. But, more importantly, I hope that you will recognize that there are options that can benefit everyone. And hopefully you will embrace peace and compassion in that knowing.

Be well,
David

When something hurtful has occurred the desire to cleanse and clear is fairly strong. By withholding empathy, suffering may actually be prolonged and more personal energy exhausted by concentrating on or avoiding someone you feel has wronged you. Regardless of your beliefs about rightness or wrongness, the doorway to forgiveness swings wide. And we all have the power to give and receive forgiveness and empathy. It takes an equal amount of compassionate understanding to graciously accept forgiveness as it does to give it.

Close your eyes for a few minutes and call to mind relationships in your life that you would truly like to move forward. See if you can name five benefits that would immediately occur if you expressed empathy and extended the hand of forgiveness. These are positive, healing thoughts; hold on to them and expand them.

The following reflection questions are related to
the Forgiveness Principle:

R | Are you more likely to practice sympathy or empathy?
E | Would you like to start fresh? In what ways?

F | What actions do you take to be authentically you? How
L | does it feel?

E |
C | Is there someone in your life who would benefit from
     | you offering forgiveness today? What's holding you
T | back?

I |
O | How have you felt when offering forgiveness to others in
     | the past?
N |
S | How does it feel when your heart is saying to offer
     | forgiveness and you don't?

CHAPTER 7:
THE LOVING UNCONDITIONALLY
PRINCIPLE

When there are disappointments or difficulties, our
abilities to express love can become very constrained.

Dear Lucia,

When you entered my world everything I thought about unconditional love changed. My emotions and senses completely overflowed the first time that I held you—a beautiful being, freshly born, created by the love between your mother and me. Until that day, I thought that babies would break if I wasn't careful enough holding them. So when I took care of you I was overly cautious and very deliberate. If we were alone for very long it created a bit of anxiety—probably for both of us. From the very beginning it seemed that you felt my love even when I did something awkwardly, like changing a diaper. In my mind I heard you say, "Try again, Daddy," and the next time I got it right.

From those very first moments I loved you even when I was filled with the uncertainties of new parenthood: sleepless nights, sickness and colic, your first smiles, and many more joys. You were and are the very essence of love.

Parents and caregivers know that a newborn will be completely dependent on them for survival. Yet there is a sense of wonder in loving a newborn that is so natural and easy. As babies grow into toddlers then school age, teens, and young adults their focus naturally flows toward self-interests. After all, babies learn from caregivers that crying, wetting, and smiling nets attention and responses. Those responses naturally fulfill babies' wants and needs—crying is soothed, wet diapers are changed, and playtime brings joy. With more life experiences comes more complexity and love often shifts from unconditional to conditional. Sometimes individuals withhold love for times when it is convenient or it meets personal expectations. When there are disappointments or we experience difficulties, our abilities for expressing love can become very constrained.

There are times, unfortunately, when interactions between people sends the message that love and acceptance are only given when things are "good." When another person lashes out in disappointment or withholds love, their actions may well have been influenced by their own internal pain or suffering. My dearest Lucia, please know that when someone's hurtful actions seemed aimed toward you, it was unlikely that you were responsible. Their inner pain may be completely hidden from you even when their harsh actions were visible.

As you grow from baby to girl to woman, it is my hope that you will stretch far beyond limiting practices and choose loving-kindness as your way of living and relating to everyone under any condition, regardless of their actions. With this as your highest intention, even though the other person may not be accepting, you will know that their momentary actions were evoked by individual perceptions of suffering. Since everyone experiences understanding in different ways, you and they may not embrace the same understanding at the same moment. However, you will be able to feel it because you will be focused on living compassionately and loving unconditionally.

I love you always and unconditionally,

Daddy

It seemed logical, if temporary, to move back to my parents' house, so I did on the last weekend of 2013. For the benefit of the family that I had been building with Jolie and Lucia, I had moved to a different county far removed from familiar surroundings, my parents, and sister. With Jolie and Lucia gone my sense of isolation would have extended by staying in our former neighborhood. I wanted to begin the healing process, so being with my parents and reconnecting with close friends would definitely help me.

According to my dad, moving back was open-ended, yet I was sensitive to overstaying or imposing. On a rainy, winter day with the help of a few of my closest friends everything but my clothes got packed into a POD. Once the unit was packed, securely locked, and ready for transport to a storage center I thanked my friends for their invaluable help, and they went on to other commitments. Then I walked through the empty apartment, pausing in each room, allowing memories of Jolie and Lucia to pour over me. Hopes, dreams, love, and excitement had filled this small apartment. My heart was overwhelmed as I recalled moving in, Jolie's pleasure at setting up Lucia's furniture, the three of us having dinner at the kitchen table, playing in the living room with Lucia, and the splashing excitement of bath time. Embracing the energy of transition, I let the memories rest then jangled the keys in my pocket and closed the door one last time. What would open up in this next stage of my life?

Before exiting the apartment community I had one last visit to make at the leasing office. Today Meredith greeted me with energetic enthusiasm, "Hi, David! Are you all packed? This is a big day for you. I'm sure that it's been tough, but I just know that things will work out for you in the future." She handed me her business card and continued, "If there is anything we can do to help you, please let me know."

"Thank you so much for all that you have done thus far. Everything is locked up, and here are the keys." Raising my hand to point outside the office window, I continued, "The POD will be picked up on Monday morning. I don't expect any issues, however, I will follow up on Monday afternoon to confirm that everything was taken off of the property smoothly. Should there be any problems, just call me."

"I will do that, David," Meredith said. Then she stood and walked around her desk, hesitantly approaching me. As she drew closer, her arms began to extend toward me. I stepped forward and wrapped my arms around her. About thirty seconds passed before we pulled back and looked into one another's tear-filled eyes.

"I needed that," I said. "Thank you for everything and be well." Meredith's kindness had helped to ease a very difficult six weeks. I turned and walked out the door and began a new journey with no intentions of returning.

An hour and a half later I arrived at my parents' house and entered through the garage. The family moved into the house in 1994, but this was my third or fourth time coming back on a temporary basis to this familiar two-story colonial. This time I wasn't a recent graduate or in a job change, instead I was an adult in the middle of a very big life change. No one was home so I walked from room to room feeling like a visitor yet comforted by familiarity. I wandered downstairs then walked the stairs to the second floor, pausing at the landing to notice framed diplomas and awards belonging to my sister and me. Just seeing them made me smile and remember the times when those milestones were achieved. At the top of the stairs was a hallway that led to a loft overlooking the family room. Adjacent to it was my sister's old room, which had been converted into a very nice guest room with brand new furniture. The nearby bathroom had been an argument zone for me and my sister in our teenage years. A short turn to the left and I was in the doorway to my old room, which was now an office for my dad with a futon, a desk, a television set, and a video game system for my nephew's visits. The blue walls and white trim were the only remnants of my teenage years. Appreciating these quiet moments, I slowly realized that I was not imposing, this was "home." My parents' support and unconditional love was a gift that I truly wanted to be open to receiving.

After a couple of weeks a routine was in place for commuting to work, preparing meals, and reconnecting with friends. I spent a good deal of time reflecting on how blessed I was to have a place to go and feel supported. It didn't matter at all whether my parents agreed with my decision to get married or with my actions while married, they practiced an unwavering love. No matter what was going on in my world, they stuck by me. Experiencing that prevailing sense of comfort allowed me to start moving forward. Lucia's birth had been my first time to express and deeply understand unconditional love. Having gradually awakened to this new awareness, I was able to recognize its essence and embrace that same type of love coming to me through my parents. Even when other supports changed or disappeared, their love has always been steady, unconditional.

I often wondered about my relationship with Lucia and how she may view me in the future. Accepting that there was a chance that I wouldn't see her for some time, I focused my attention on loving her now and minimized my worries about things I had no control over or what she might perceive based on stories she could have been told.

When I meditated I envisioned the last times we were together, remembering pure sweetness, an innocent baby girl always glowing with joy. For a full month during my daily meditations I visualized her growing up and experiencing life. I saw myself walking her to the bus stop and helping her onto the bus for her first day of kindergarten. And then I pictured a few years later, and the two of us having dinner together. She was ecstatic about the new things she had learned in school that day. In one experience the two of us were wearing all white, facing one another and sitting in a beautiful garden meditating together. She had grown tall like I am, and her hair was long and flowing like her mother's. I could feel her excitement and pleasure to be spending time with me. Then I envisioned her at sixteen and starting to date. Like many parents I disagreed with some of her choices, and she became upset with me and walked away. In the last Lucia vision that I had that month, I responded to a knock at the door and opened it to see Lucia standing there. When my eyes met hers we both began to cry. Every image felt like future premonitions. The love that I felt the day that Lucia was born has permeated all of the times I have experienced her in meditation, and I easily equate those feelings with the love that my parents have expressed to me. It seems natural to experience and demonstrate unconditional love for a child, to an elder, or anyone with whom you have shared a deep bond. Extending untethered loving-kindness out to the world, including those with whom you have had conflict, is the full expression of unconditional love. As my understanding deepened, I was able to extend that same love to Jolie and truly feel that the highest good in me recognizes and honors the highest good in her. I perceived the false fear and anxiety that had captured Jolie, and my most compassionate feelings and intentions sent unconditional love toward her.

On the day that marked four agonizing months since Jolie fled the country with my daughter, I slept with my phone right beside me ready to check for messages. An anticipative sense developed in me hoping to wake up to a message from Jolie.

With everything continuing in crisis mode, I made small efforts toward keeping weekend routines. My habit was to wake up early, quickly clear miscellaneous messages, and then go back to sleep. But today sleep didn't take over, and I awoke three times before dawn. The third time there was an e-mail from Jolie, startling and filling me with anxiety and a twinge of nausea. After four long months, what was prompting her to contact me now? I had sent e-mails on top of e-mails trying in vain to establish communication, and my last message was well over a month ago. My mind jittered with anticipation—maybe e-mail deliveries to her had been delayed. I did—and did not— want to read her e-mail. Taking several rapid breaths then pushing one long breath out, I collected myself and tapped the iPhone screen, bringing Jolie's message into view.

> *Hi, David,*
>
> *I hope you and your family are doing well. I am writing you this letter to inform you that I have used your credit card to pay off an important bill and unfreeze an account. Here in my country, I found a job that requires verification of my education. If you wouldn't put Lucia and me in this situation, I wouldn't have left the U.S.*

As I read line after line of the e-mail my small reserve of energy seemed to drain into a pool of exasperation. Since we had agreed to divorce about a month before Jolie left the country, I had removed her name from my credit cards, so it was quite a surprise that the charge would have gone through. But the most startling, painful part of the e-mail was her declaration to truly keep Lucia away from me. If she was able to obtain full-time employment in another country and earn enough to provide for herself and Lucia, the chances of reuniting with my daughter were slim to none. There was nothing I could do at this early hour, so I calmed and soothed myself like an infant and slept.

At 7:00 a.m. I rose to start my day. Breakfast was a bowl of cereal, which I ate sitting on the living room couch while rereading Jolie's early morning e-mail.

> *I couldn't let you have full custody of Lucia. Since coming here, Lucia has continued the therapy that we started last summer. I have spent all the money I had on her therapies and just found a good job that will pay me enough to cover additional therapy and our living expenses. She can now walk and can say a couple of words. Since we couldn't find this type of treatment in the U.S., it is not in my plans to come back.*
>
> *Overall, David, all I need is your help right now. Once I start earning money, I'll repay you over time. Also, you can file your taxes and file for divorce on your own. You do not need my signature. Hopefully you will understand my situation. All that I'm doing now is for Lucia. I'll do anything for her.*
>
> *Be well,*
> *Jolie*

Feeling like an enormous boulder had rolled on top of my head and shoulders, I leaned against the chair padding to relieve the pressure. Jolie's determination had not changed, and I felt that no wounds had been healed during our time apart. In her opinion, I'm the bad guy forcing her to enact this decision. Pictures of the beginning of discord in our relationship began floating through my mind then slammed shut on the day she left with Lucia. We never saw eye to eye on treatment for Lucia's torticollis, a very treatable condition in infants. Some of the best hospitals in the country are accessible and nearby. Jolie didn't seem to be open to those options because she didn't like the overall healthcare system in the U.S. It didn't help that our local pediatricians had not identified the torticollis; instead Jolie recognized many early symptoms and almost forced the diagnosis. At times we were just waiting for referrals to specialists, and the time lag for appointments only prolonged management of Lucia's situation. As a result, Jolie saw taking Lucia abroad as the only viable alternative. In her mind her rationale was justified, although it did not resonate with me because local treatments were readily available. One thing was clear, Jolie's love for Lucia was deep and unwavering.

I was confused about what Jolie truly needed. It was certain that she had already used my credit card, but it was unclear whether she intended to return after Lucia's treatments concluded and what other financial support she might want. Maybe all she was trying to do was get medical help for Lucia in a system that she understood. I wanted to believe that was true.

To keep dialogue open and attain some clarity, my e-mail reply was simple, asking only for clarification.

> Hi, Jolie,
> Do you plan to return once Lucia's treatments are done? What is it that you need my help with?
>
> David

While I awaited her reply I accessed my credit card account, checking for transactions. As of that morning two authorizations had taken place in excess of $4000.00, both related to the account that Jolie had referenced. There was little time for anger. Because normal authorizations post to a credit card account after two or three days my goal was to race against the clock and ensure that payment to the merchant did not happen. If it were to post it would mean that the merchant had been paid, and the hold would have been lifted giving Jolie the account access that she sought. I had no way of validating Jolie's intentions, but I did know that access to the account would continue to keep Lucia away from me.

My efforts began by calling the credit card company's 800 number and speaking with a customer service representative. I explained that my soon-to-be ex-wife had fled the country, taken my daughter, and used my card without permission and that I wanted the charges blocked as fraudulent. In hindsight, I probably gave many more details than I should have. The customer service representative recommended that I call the merchant directly to inquire if they would be willing to delete the authorization. Making multiple calls and repeating painful details was incredibly stressful, made more so by a sinking sensation that Lucia was slipping through my fingers with each passing second. It would have been easy to pour all of my frustration and anger onto the customer service representative because she couldn't help me. But that would have been unfair to her and a misguided use of my own energy. Instead I took a deep breath and headed for the shower. I had forty-eight hours to make something happen and turn things around.

The next morning, I was awakened by another e-mail from Jolie. She responded to my request for clarification on what resources she needed and her plans to return to the U.S.

> *David,*
> *As of now all I need is the money to pay off the account so I can access needed information for job applications. So if you can wait for reimbursement, I will gradually repay you as I said in my previous e-mail.*
>
> *Jolie*

How could she ask me to pay her account and enable her to remain out of the country with my daughter? Her request was unbelievable! I did not hesitate to send a response.

> *Jolie,*
> *I do not authorize you to use my credit card, and I do not agree with you continuing to keep Lucia away from me.*
>
> *David*

Since I didn't expect an immediate response from Jolie, I outlined tasks for the remainder of the day, the first item being to apprise the merchant of the full situation and halt Jolie's plan by tomorrow.

After combing the merchant's website for names of decision makers I crafted a message to six individuals, carefully choosing my words to express the seriousness and urgency of my inquiry. I apologized for contacting them directly and revealed that my wife had abducted our daughter and left the U.S. in early November 2013. Then I confirmed working with an attorney and local, national, and international authorities to exercise all options. I informed them that my estranged wife had used my credit card without my authorization to pay an outstanding debt to their organization, and I requested that the transaction be halted and the account put on hold. I also expressed my willingness to meet in person with any decision makers on Monday. I repeated the urgency of the situation and sincerely thanked them for their consideration and immediate attention. One of the organization's officers responded and advised me that my inquiry had been forwarded to their legal counsel.

Clear skies on Monday morning introduced a sense of optimism tinged with anxiety. Another e-mail arrived from Jolie regarding my disapproval of her use of my credit card. How could this be when I was the one left alone and childless? The instant that question pierced my thoughts a sensation moved through me, and I began to experience a shift in perspective. Reading her emotion-filled words, I began to relate to her sense of victimization and the way that she viewed me as the instigator.

> *David,*
> *To be honest I actually expected this reaction from you. I don't care whether you authorize anything or support anything at all. You should be happy that I left you. Don't spend your life trying to get Lucia back because I assure you that you have zero chance of seeing her again. I understand the laws and have read case studies. I spent enough money to make sure that you won't get her back, EVER. If we return to the U.S., Lucia will be taken from me. I will not lose my daughter.*

Lucia is my life, and I'd rather die than lose her.

Anyway, I have no more time for you. So it is pointless to continue to write. Sending you light and love from a sunnyside land.

Jolie

The sarcasm in her closing words clearly mocked my spiritual journey because Jolie would not use words like "light" and "love," nor did they align with her intentions. But she was correct that my priorities were different from hers. Rather than replying, I forwarded our e-mail exchanges to my attorney so that he would understand Jolie's intentions regarding finances and Lucia's custody.

Midway through the morning while at work I took a break, left my office, and checked my credit card balance and was very happy to see that the charge had not posted to the account. I called the merchant's billing office to explain about unauthorized charges on my credit card account. Since I was calling about Jolie's personal account the customer service representative politely told me that she could not help me. Holding on to a thin thread of confidence I said, "I understand that there are certain rules. Please let me explain what is going on, and hopefully you will be able to put me in touch with the right people." I unraveled Lucia's abduction and Jolie's use of my credit card and the advice of my credit card company that only the merchant could request deletion of pending charges.

Doing just as she was trained to do, the representative told me that she was sorry about my situation but unable to help me. When I disconnected and laid the phone down, my neck bent forward and my face fell into my empty palms. My shoulders sagged and the center of my body folded forward, caught by bending arms and elbows bumping the top of a small table. It took every ounce of my energy not to start shaking all over.

In the next five minutes the common area at my workplace filled with passersby, so I relocated to a nearby conference room to be alone with my thoughts and pull myself together. I felt like an animated movie character holding back collapsing steel walls and shrieking about being crushed. My thoughts whirred around. "There has to be another way." Time was racing by. It was 3:00 p.m. and none of yesterday's contacts had replied. Should I reach out to my own network of friends who worked for my credit card company? As fast as I could discern keypad letters, I sent text messages to two good friends who were incredibly knowledgeable of credit card systems and also had networks of advisors.

My text read, "I need your help, it's an emergency!" In less than sixty seconds my phone vibrated with a reply from Rita, one of the kindest and gentlest souls I have ever met. For over thirteen years we have been close contacts, each highly respecting the other. "I'm in a bit of a bind," I said, "and hoping you will lead me in the right direction. If anyone can help, I know you can."

Rita responded, "You know I will do my best."

I kept in touch with several professional contacts, but personal life details were seldom exchanged. So I gave Rita a five-minute overview. She explained that she would be unable to facilitate my request, however, she referred me to a former colleague of hers whom I also knew. Since my window of opportunity was closing down, I cut my conversation short in favor of making the next call.

Just the sound of Dottie's familiar voice was comforting, and I sucked in a big gulp of air and began, "I'm calling to ask a huge favor on an urgent personal matter." With both empathy and authority in her voice, Dottie began outlining options for getting the charge reversed. As I prepared to read the account number to her I saw an incoming e-mail from my attorney. So I alerted Dottie and temporarily put her on hold.

> *David,*
> *I just heard from the merchant's attorney. A hold has been put on her account, but the attorney did not know if the information she had requested had been released. In the meantime, I advised him about the orders entered by the court.*
>
> *Best,*
> *Aaron*

Toggling back into my conversation with Dottie, I said, "It looks like the transaction has been blocked. I just received an e-mail from my attorney. Wow, I can't believe the timing of all of this! Thank you very much for your willingness to help. I really appreciate you!"

"Let me know if there is anything I can do to help," she replied. "Good luck with everything."

I finally exhaled, releasing seventy-two hours of whirling anxiety. Though I was no closer to being with my daughter, the fact that communication was rolling forward really increased my optimism. I realized that a feeling of empathy and unconditional love for Jolie was gradually increasing within me. Even though her last e-mail was angry and resolved to keep Lucia away, my sense of compassion was taking hold. She was far removed from seeing my vantage point, but my dominant intention was to hold her in a positive light because I loved her the same way that my parents loved me and the way that I loved Lucia, unconditionally.

The Loving Unconditionally Principle

When multiple events, worries, and decisions pelt down like an afternoon thunderstorm, the ability to respond with loving-kindness or compassion can be hampered or completely suppressed. Relief is what anyone would want and might do almost anything to achieve it.

After four months of silence, receiving e-mails from Jolie about accessing a credit card to pay off a personal debt triggered an intense three-day period of unmanageable emotions, bouncing up and down, back and forth. On Saturday I was hopeful, by Sunday pessimism prevailed, then Monday debuted frustration. Anger and defensiveness arose when I felt personally attacked. Anxiety, suffering, and confusion traveled head to toe, limb to limb.

Because I had recently accessed the Compassion Principle those negative emotions did not take hold. A shift in my energy and receptivity had already taken place, and I was incredibly grateful. I was in a more allowing state and ready to receive the feelings of comfort that gradually moved through me, revealing that no matter how hurtful things were, or how Jolie felt about me, I loved her in the same unconditional way that I love Lucia. This sensation of compassionate, unconditional love was unrelated to marriage or "being in love." Instead it was for Jolie, a human being overcome with fear and suffering.

Like light filtering through a gauzy curtain, a small ray shone through. Had I sensed desperation in Jolie's reply e-mail? Was she afraid or uncertain? For a flickering moment I extracted my emotions from the crisis and became the observer able to recognize that Jolie's fear was as large as mine. Just this subtle awareness revealed more evidence of the internal shift that was advancing within me. In that clarifying moment, I recognized that fear of losing custody of Lucia, feeling overwhelmed, and a belief in limited options propelled Jolie into the decision to take Lucia. Since I can't replicate the intensity of her fears, I am not able to feel what she felt. Yet I know that I would not have made the same decision. My newly found awareness is that what seems rational, or irrational, to one person might be perceived as the complete opposite to another person. This shift in perspective was one of the most profoundly freeing experiences I have ever had.

To express unconditional love is to keep love flowing from and through yourself, not choking it off because of difficult circumstances. The act of purposefully withholding loving-kindness only produces more pain; therefore, it is as positive for the giver as for the receiver.

By using the power of our imaginations to consider how others may be feeling or motivated, we enter into empathy, which opens the door to compassion. Compassion leads the way into unconditional love, and the power to focus automatically doubles. The more aware and purposeful you become in setting your intentions toward the highest good, the greater the flow of unconditional love to you and through you.

The following reflection questions are related to
the Loving Unconditionally Principle:

R

E What have you wanted "relief" from today or sometime
this week?

F

L When you think of loving someone unconditionally,
who immediately comes to mind?

E

C In what ways have you found fault with someone close
to you? Have you chosen to release it? How have you

T felt since then?

I

O Do you have relationships where you give love when
it feels convenient? What stops you from loving those

N individuals all the time?

S

How would your life improve if you gave and received
love unconditionally to everyone you encountered?

CHAPTER 8:
THE GRATITUDE PRINCIPLE

Life challenges are often sudden, surprising,
and even frightening;
we are not always quick to see them as opportunities.

Dear Lucia,

As I write this letter we have been apart for eighteen long months, and each day I hope and pray that we will soon be reunited. Every month has tested me in ways that I never imagined. Prior to the time that we were separated I had never dealt with any major life traumas. So I've been blessed in that regard. The experience of suddenly being separated from you has often felt surreal, and I repeatedly shot questions out to the greater universe asking why it was happening to me. Then you appeared to me in a dream telling me that everything would be okay. That beautiful dream brought forward an inspiring new perspective. Rather than happening "to me," could it be happening "for me"?

Since life challenges are often sudden, surprising, and even frightening we are not always quick to see them as opportunities. Amazingly, we continue to expand with every experience, including harsh challenges. All of these aspects of ourselves enlarge: knowing, skills, understanding, awareness, and more. We seem to be "new," emerging from each experience, and that, my dear, is one of the most intriguing aspects of life. At the very center of living is the conscious expansion of who we are. Each of us is completely in charge of the labels that we put on our experiences—good or bad, wanted or unwanted. Each experience fuels our expansion, which shapes our perspective. When your awareness revs up and you deeply know that you are in moments of expansion, gratitude pours in, and you may even be inspired to share with others.

I want you to know that I hold all that has happened in the last eighteen months in a space of gratitude. Someone else might misinterpret my words and believe that I am "happy" for the trauma, but that is not at all what I mean. My gratitude is born out of focusing on a larger picture and greater good unfolding—a greater good for so many more than just you and me, my angel.

I have been writing letters to you about choosing to live purposefully and the principles that I have been privileged to experience and understand. The principle that embraces all of the others is gratitude. When feelings of acceptance and compassion are missing then it is almost impossible to sincerely express gratitude.

Writing this book has been a way for me to express my love for you and channel positive energy to you. With all of my heart, I truly hope that one day you will be able to read each page and feel how much you have been loved and continue to be loved by me.

Moreover, I hope you will learn to look at life experiences in multiple ways and recognize that a short-term unhappiness could evolve into a significant long-term goodness for you and many others. Setting your intention to purposefully look through the lens of gratitude is the ultimate tribute to the human experience.

As you grow, my angel, know that you are lacking nothing, and make it your intention to practice gratitude for all that has already been given. The love that I have for you transcends the thousands of miles and the many hours that we have been apart. Just like the air that you breathe, I am always with you.

I love you always and forever,

Daddy

It has been more than a year since I last heard from Jolie. And during my time of separation from Lucia, I've yet to see a new picture or hear her speak. I never wanted to press charges, nor will I. That approach feels retaliatory and fueled with negativity, which creates more fear in my opinion. I am very grateful that a friend referred me to a law firm in Uzbekistan that is willing to represent me and help to get my custody order recognized in the Uzbek courts. My goal is to be an active part of Lucia's life experience, not to separate mother and daughter. I continue to feel a deep, abiding connection to Lucia and experience her essence in dreams and meditation.

In amazing ways this painful, difficult trauma has served as a catalyst for my awakening, and I am profoundly grateful for being able to experience the world through clearer eyes and with a more open heart. It is my highest intention to be open to all possibilities for reuniting with my daughter and to hold a space of compassion for everyone who has been impacted by these traumatic events, including Jolie. Through these experiences I have begun to live a new perspective that will, hopefully, sow seeds of inspiration for others. Many, many people have and will have challenging life situations, all equally significant. Each of us sees and feels through the eyes of self. I urge you to be compassionate toward yourself, and know that no matter what you are experiencing, wanted or unwanted, everything can change in an instant. In fact, it will change as your perspective changes and evolves. Think of this as the lens of choice. You are completely in charge of the manner in which you view your situations and the type of energy you pour into them. They are not exclusive to you. Both your perceptions and emotional energies are projecting into your immediate environment and out to the world.

Ponder this question: How would everything look and feel if you purposefully practiced mindfulness and openness and channeled every intention through the very essence of loving-kindness? As your journeys continue, please carry my heartfelt thoughts with you.

"When we begin to view all of our experiences through the lens of gratitude, our heart, mind, and spirit naturally expand."
—David

The Gratitude Principle

Since I was a young boy I remember hearing the often-used phrase, "Count your blessings." As that young boy, I thought that blessings were the tangible "things" that I had. During holidays or birthdays I was eager to receive something I really wanted: a toy, video game, or a new bicycle. I didn't understand that those material things were made possible through my family's sacrifice and hard work. When I began working to support myself and acquire things my understanding shifted, yet my definition of gratitude still centered on material abundance. The trauma of being separated from my daughter and awakening to purposeful living has moved my perception of gratitude farther than a rotation around the sun! My awareness has vaulted from material to experiential and significantly expanded as a result of experiences that I would have previously defined as "bad" or "negative."

A deepening sense of gratitude seems to create a parallel path for humility. We begin to see the goodness in everything and the beauty of universal order. It is comforting and soothing to view all that has already happened through the lens of gratitude and to open your arms in eager appreciation of what is yet to come.

Have you ever sat and thought about the experiences that you are most grateful for? Were they positive or negative? For many of us emotions are on overdrive when going through something profoundly negative. When you choose the role of observer and purposefully set emotions aside, individual experiences become opportunities for gratitude and deep learning. Emotional responses, low or high, are temporary. I've made the commitment to try to disconnect my emotions from situations that don't feel good, and when I am successful, the healing is lightning quick, as is the downshift in anxiety. Empathy and gratitude prevail and carry me through the moment and onward. I hope that you will strive for the same good feelings as your journeys continue.

May peace and love be your constant companions and my sincere hopes for your continued well-being.

The following reflection questions are related to
the Gratitude Principle:

R E F L E C T I O N S

When you were ten what were the top three things that you were grateful for? When you were twenty-one? What are the top three things on your gratitude list today?

Many people believe that in every life lesson there is something to be learned. Think of a time that you went through something very difficult. What was the lesson that you learned from that experience? Now take a current negative experience and think to yourself: Is there a lesson that is being learned here?

During your growing-up years when you were prompted to "count your blessings," what was your response? Your gut-level response?

Who and what do you value the most today? In what ways are you valued by others?

CHAPTER 9:
PRINCIPLES AND PRACTICES

"A disciplined mind leads to happiness, and an
undisciplined mind leads to suffering."
—Dalai Lama, XIV

*I*n this special chapter I have brought all of the principles together in shorter versions so that they can become yours. By combining these summaries with the reflection questions from each chapter, my hope is that this combination will enhance your ability to apply the principles in areas of your life where you'd like to see improvement. Being honest with ourselves is often difficult. But it's the fundamental basis for finding your path to peace and working through difficult circumstances. I encourage you to continue to keep your intentions focused on an improvement in your well-being. You are already better off!

In addition to the condensed principles, I've also included some practices that have been instrumental to maintaining my sense of balance throughout this experience. If you decide to explore any of these practices further, I'm optimistic that you will see the benefit of integrating them into your life.

The Heart Principle

Focusing and feeling my way through negative or fearful mental commentaries nets different results than analysis. Leading with my heart rather than my head has proved to be an amazing, fulfilling way to experience the world!

Although I experienced some initial fear when Jolie told me she was pregnant, I was also very excited about having a family. I had grown up in a loving home, and the desire for my own family was prominent.

Today I rely on my intuition and internal compass, and when

I veer off course, I am alert to the resistance and redirect as soon as I can. Stepping back and observing situations rather than becoming heatedly, emotionally enmeshed has been the single best way to determine whether my mind or heart is in charge. Try getting excited about the fresh newness of each moment, hour, and day and the continuing shifts in perspectives.

If you want to ignite your own expansion, I sincerely encourage you to pursue true freedom by quieting your mind and opening your heart.

The Awareness Principle

As we move around in our daily lives we literally bump into other peoples' experiences, and they into ours. If you have been aware of this, have you ever stopped to consider someone else's level of awareness and presence in a given moment? What if each of us took the position that most of the time everyone is trying to manage multiple situations and doing the best that they can? And what if we lit up a lot of dark corners by shining the light of compassionate understanding toward everyone we encountered?

When Ami stayed with us the week after Lucia's birth I exhibited behaviors that flashed back to my early childhood. Our life experiences are our profound teachers, and I was able to meet that lesson when Jolie's words helped me see myself through Ami's side of our joint experience. As that new awareness charged through me, I was startled and embarrassed. That awareness was incredibly powerful!

There is great clarity to be gained from recognizing that we are only able to control our own individual responses and not circumstances. Awareness is the leading edge of awakening.

The Intention Principle

An intention toward an outcome forms once we have defined a perception and taken a stand (attitude) on it. If I observe a situation and instantly label it as "difficult," I might jump in to muscle my way through without even pausing to evaluate.

However, there's an equal opportunity to step back and observe before assigning any labels or expending any negative energy.

Spending a few seconds revising an initial perception and setting a new intention can literally transform "difficult" to "smooth." We have the power to change our perceptions and attitudes because we initiate and control them. To have any hope of controlling them, we must first become aware and develop a sincere honesty with ourselves about their creation and their impermanence.

I continue to delve into my own thoughts and the intentions behind them, embracing the practice of mindfulness. When I am centered and mindful, shaping intentions takes on a whole new form. And when you are inspired to project positive intentions you are more likely to influence shifts in perceptions and outcomes for others in your environment. There is no doubt that my Reiki experience and deepening meditations have broadened my understanding about the power of intention in all of us and the role of openness and sincere belief in the possibilities.

The Acceptance Principle

During the five days between Jolie's frightening e-mail and confirmation of their overseas flight, I allowed my life to be overtaken with puzzling, impossible questions. I lost touch, and then two excruciating weeks later I stopped protesting and raised my own flag of surrender, accepting that I was unable to control these circumstances. Only my emotions and responses were in my control.

Practicing the principle of acceptance is not the same as giving up or giving in. Instead, it means to calmly stop arguing the "if onlys" and "but whys." Imagine that a favorite bowl slipped out of your hands, hit the floor, and broke into five pieces. Even though you could glue the pieces together, turning the clock back and stopping the crash to the floor is unlikely. The immediate or distant past is unchangeable by you in this present moment.

In that spectacular moment of acceptance, I released any feelings of being a victim of the situation and embraced the most amazing source of strength and positivity that I had ever known. Compassion for Jolie, Lucia, and everyone around me streamed from head to toe. As profoundly negative as it was for Jolie to leave with Lucia, there was an equal possibility of future abundant joy.

The Compassion Principle

Until the day of Lucia's abduction and my aunt's passing I had never had to manage an earthquake-like jolt in my world. Anger, upset, embarrassment, shame, and resentment surged through me. But in the early morning dream and reoccurrence in meditation when I saw Lucia, an amazing release transpired, and I was filled with peace, understanding, and compassion. My conditioned responses fell away, and this profound new experience became the cornerstone to my awakening.

I have steadfastly embraced this principle of compassion, experiencing the most inspiring feelings I have ever known! My inner and outer space has become a "humanity zone" with rising levels of compassion. It is a central part of being human to want to relate to and see ourselves through others. Seeing through the eyes of self, myself and yourself, is our primary lens to life. Our view of self and others shifts as we become more aware and awake. Embracing the principle of compassion has given me new eyes and new perspective. Now if I am asked to choose sides, my first thought is to consider two or more viewpoints. Taking a few moments to recognize and honor another's situation may initiate your own shift in perspective. This is a key ingredient for living purposefully, which will alter your own giving and receiving of life energy. My eyes and senses feel vibrant and new, and my compassionate heart continues to strengthen.

The Forgiveness Principle

When you or I withhold empathy our suffering may actually be prolonged, and more energy may be wasted debating the rightness or wrongness of things that have already transpired and moved far beyond our control. My desire for inner peace was so very strong that it pushed me toward realizing that it would be unachievable until I had released my anxiety and anger toward Jolie and entered into a space of empathy and forgiveness.

The sender of empathy and forgiveness benefits as much, or more, than the receiver because it initiates a cleansing effect for both parties. Accepting or rejecting forgiveness cannot be forced. By setting aside beliefs about rightness or wrongness, compassionate understanding becomes the key to opening the doorway to forgiveness. Since we know that we are in charge of our emotions and responses, we also hold the power buttons to generate opportunities to move forward and to create a forgiving environment.

Every time I recall the dream when Lucia whispered to me, "Everything's going to be okay, Daddy," I am comforted and infused with the pleasure of giving and receiving forgiveness.

The Loving Unconditionally Principle

My newly found awareness is that someone else's definition of logical or illogical may be the polar opposite of mine, therefore, our perceptions differ. When existing in the state of unawareness individuals can become completely overcome with fear and suffering and exhibit behaviors that are surprising and alarming. Perpetuating thoughts that find fault with others suppresses positive energy and reduces well-being. Unrelated to marriage or "being in love," the practice of compassionate, unconditional love does not mean to ignore or look away from hurtful people or situations. Instead, this is a powerful reminder for the giver of the love not to choke your own natural, loving nature in response to someone else's behavior. With this flash of insight, I now know to focus my intentions on acting in loving-kindness.

To feel empathetic one must use imagination to consider how others may be feeling or motivated. Having accessed empathy, compassion is nearby and leads the way into unconditional love. Regardless of people or circumstances, let it be your highest and most continuous intention to center yourself and live through loving-kindness and unconditional love for yourself and extending to all others. Whisper to yourself, "I am they, and they are me."

The Gratitude Principle

In our earliest childhood experiences we often link gratitude to things, yet over time our awareness shifts, and we realize feelings rather than things increase joy. You probably agree with prominent authors and researchers who have found that choosing to live in thankfulness is the gateway to greater healthiness and that practicing gratitude is a fantastic stress buster!

Perhaps you benefitted from a wise grandparent or teacher who regularly said, "Count your blessings." But it really has nothing to do with keeping a check list or counting to two hundred. Instead, it is about the depth of feeling derived from giving to and receiving from the world around you, and especially those you hold dear. In an insightful moment or in complete stillness, such as meditation, we are very likely to realize the influences of people, even traumatic situations, on our personal expansions. In other words, we didn't get to where we are by ourselves.

What is the physical sensation of being in a state of gratitude? Imagine how your body feels after working out or spending an hour bending and scrubbing. Then you take a warm shower, put on clean clothes, and sip a glass of tea. Right in that moment when warmth and satisfaction is palpable in your whole body— you are oozing with gratitude sensations. In the state of gratitude we connect more deeply with others and raise our estimates of the ways in which we value and are valued. Practicing gratitude is like a heat strip in the center of your body, warming your whole being and radiating out to all with whom you interact.

Meaningful Practices

As I approached the completion of this book, I reflected on understandings and practices that have introduced comfort and balance: meditation, openness, and self-love. A deep, innate part of me believes that what I've experienced is for the purpose of emerging into the person that I have always wanted to be: heart centered, aware, accepting, intentional, compassionate, forgiving, loving, and grateful. Prior to experiencing this expansion, my own understanding of how these principles were showing up for me was very new, immature, and limited. When I practiced forgiveness it was at my own convenience. I only expressed gratitude for things I defined as "good" or "abundant." Embracing these principles has shifted my way of being so that I consciously view all experiences through the lens of these principles no matter how polarizing I may perceive situations in a given moment. I can only hope that these experiences have also initiated similar shifts for individuals closest to me. As Mahatma Gandhi said, "Be the change you want to see in the world." And I am recognizing that my desire to "be" the change is the fire starter for becoming more alert and aware of all of my interactions. Although my situation may appear to be unique, many others have or are also in the midst of significant shifts in ways of being and perspective. Some ease into their awakenings, while others are catapulted forward by adversity. No matter the timing or the vehicle, our unwavering destination is expansion.

In addition to discovering these eight principles for purposeful living, I have experienced significant breakthroughs in other aspects of my life. When I opened my heart to more meaning and depth everything accelerated. There were many unique moments when I fully recognized that I had envisioned and asked for these changes. A shower of synchronicities appeared in my life evidenced by situations and people providing deep insights and new perspectives. Soon I was not baffled by the changes taking place, instead I realized that this was the new life I had imagined. Close friends and family didn't necessarily understand all of these shifts, but they noticed a difference in me. I had a new perspective marked and illuminated by an increasingly open heart. Several new practices have become sturdy pillars supporting my expansion. These practices are very complementary to the principles and have inspired and sweetened my expansion and source of peace.

MEDITATION

The practice of meditation was initially introduced to me by new friends. I am forever grateful for the clearing effect that it has created in me. It has become my daily practice, and through it I feel much more grounded and balanced. In the nonjudgmental stillness of meditation I release the accumulation of thoughts and experiences of any given day and simply let go. I am able to enjoy a sense of liberation and renewal and view each day as a positive opportunity because I am releasing old, stale energy. Endeavoring to find a middle way, achieving a neutral position, has helped me to look at situations less judgmentally and with expanding compassion. As a result, the world around me just seems to flow more easily.

Distractions flowing in and out of each day can become overwhelming for many of us, complicating a harmonious space between professional and personal priorities. Emotions vacillate as we carry energy from one to another spilling out unwelcome disruptions (i.e. work to home). To minimize that potential, I immediately take fifteen minutes upon entering my home to sit, focus solely on breathing, and clear my energy from the day. My clearing meditations are simply visualization exercises. Once I close my eyes and am clear and present for a few moments, I imagine a radiant, white light pouring into the top of my head, progressing all the way down to my toes. When the light reaches my feet, I envision every emotion or negative thought within me at that moment streaming out of my feet and dispersing down into the earth. I've found that this practice serves to switch my emotions and energy from "daily stress" to "neutral state" before I begin workdays or evenings at home. In a similar fashion, I wake up a few minutes early and organize morning activities so that I can reserve fifteen minutes to meditate prior to leaving home. If the fifteen-minute meditation does not happen, I do a shorter centering meditation during my commute to work (walking or via train) or before starting full-scale office activities. The main emphasis is to save the time, honor the time, and make it a daily practice. I don't want to bring tense personal energy into the workplace or to my work family. When I have left work, I want to interact positively with family and friends and make it a priority to be fully alert in their presence.

Leading research confirms that there are significant benefits to making meditation a regular part of our lives. Growing up I thought that meditation didn't fit my belief system. It felt very "woo woo" or mystical. In its simplest form, meditation is a practice of releasing spinning, colliding thoughts and just being centered and present. Once you begin to protect these few precious minutes each day and honor your highest good by centering and being present, you will be amazed at how uncluttered your mind becomes. I was amazed, and you will be too, at the powerful clarity that comes through. How I have personally benefited from meditation goes far beyond the few words I am sharing here. To find and hold a space of peace, joy, and gratitude in smooth or rough times and purposefully release unwanted and draining emotional energy is a benefit so large that I cannot even do it justice.

OPENNESS

This journey for me began with my desire to be open and nonjudgmental toward whatever is presented in the next and next moments. Even though I questioned many things, the old David embraced the mental models that he grew up with. When I didn't "know that I knew," I have believed that there are no accidents and that all happenings are part of a meaningful inner workings. I recognized and am delighted by universal order in motion, witnessing small miracles, unexpected job offers, and connections to new avenues that will help me reunite with my daughter. The Latin origin of the word miracle is "mirari," which means "to wonder," which is just what I am doing as I am becoming more and more open. Our minds can assign limitations through the perceptions that we practice. Awareness to all other possibilities gradually dissolves when we become conditioned to certain beliefs or hold on to singular perspectives. Only in these difficult eighteen months have I truly embraced and appreciated this understanding. In my compassionate and hopeful heart, I want to believe that anything is possible, yet being only one individual, I am not likely to envision with any certainty the full universal perspective in all of its complexity and constant change. In moments that are particularly challenging it's easy to become convinced of severe restrictions and zero options. Emerging from those trying circumstances—and we do—we are transformed, we have expanded. Multiple chances and guesses are pushed out of the way by transformation.

What if your navigation skills were so keen that every interaction and experience of your journey matched your highest desires? Be open to that possibility because you are in charge of setting and removing perceived limitations. What if where you want to be and what you want to do are unclear today? That's perfectly okay. Don't worry that you must nail down an ultimate, final direction today. Instead, just commit to spending dedicated time in stillness several times every week, feeling through your thoughts until a few things repeat or float to the top. Feel the ease of knowing that you are only choosing for now and what you know right now. Developing ways to express your hopes and desires is as important as getting on the highway and knowing the direction to drive to reach an appointment. Without targets, even short term ones, almost all circumstances become difficult to manage. However, if you encourage your own good feelings, express gratitude, and become more open to the unfolding path synchronicities will flow right to you. As you become more alert and aware of new opportunities, the universe will positively reinforce you every time. You will be "feeling" the flow from your heart space as I mentioned earlier.

Think about being really hungry and walking into a restaurant teeming with delicious scents and spices. Your eager receptivity almost guarantees enjoying the meal. By becoming open and allowing, we create a receiving bay for the desires that initiated more openness. When you began reading this book, if you were thirsty for purposeful living, you may have felt instantly connected to what is being shared on the pages. It could ebb and flow as you read more pages or you could have totally disconnected. How open you are, or endeavor to be, is one of the biggest influencers to hearing and seeing things that trigger and reinforce messages in this book, and all other experiences in your life. In your new openness you will become keenly aware that exciting things are happening and that you are expanding.

SELF-CARE

This traumatic life experience has taught me the importance of caring for the self. The only thing I truly have control over is my perception of my experiences. I cannot and should not want to force someone else to embrace my points of view. Unfortunately, many of us spend a tremendous amount of energy trying to convince others to see the world our way. If someone is open to things I have said and it resonates with them, their feelings and/ or knowledge will expand about that subject. However, if they are more closed and my words have not resonated with them, any further attempts on my part to shift their views will stall out. Railing against someone else's viewpoints that happen to be different from mine is likely to deflate my own positive energy.

Albert Einstein said, "Energy endures and cannot be created or destroyed; it can only be changed from one form to another."

So, with that in mind, I urge you to endeavor to explore the depth of who you are and repurpose your own energy to clarify the pathway to your own personal truth. Removing protective behaviors and masks and becoming truly interested in and exploring self-understanding is ultra critical to maintaining peace and joy throughout your life. We have all experienced negative and positive sensations from judging others or being judged. To release the negative aspect of judging and maintain a strong connection with humanity and your individuality, make forgiving and accepting your primary way of being. Eliminate the practice of judging others who see things differently than you do; it is just different, not necessarily wrong or harmful. Send loving-kindness to yourself and be patient as you work to make this change.

In order to send positive energy into your immediate environment and out into the world, you must feel good about yourself. It is almost impossible to give positivity to others when you are sad, mad, or feeling depleted. Even though you might try to disguise your emotions by putting on a "poker face," the truth of your feelings still resides in your heart. Our feelings are just that—feelings—coming and going. And we are all allowed to feel the way that we do. Your greatest benefits will come from being very honest with yourself and nurturing, forgiving, and eliminating negative judgments. Specific actions that we take based on feelings are a different matter because those actions may encroach on others. Meditation is a powerful vehicle for exploring feelings and reasoning and pursuing deeper understanding of "whats" and "whys." It is a primary step in truly caring for yourself, even if it feels a bit self-centered at first. We can only see (experience) through the eyes of "self," myself and yourself, and accordingly, we tend to practice what we believe and distribute it through our words and actions. Pause a minute and ask yourself if you have been affirming or disaffirming. Consider investing in yourself and spend some beneficial, "selfish" time exploring your central beliefs and values and what you truly believe about yourself.

SELF-LOVE

As a teenager I was a bit of a hopeless romantic, dreaming about experiencing true love. My affection for compelling lyrics and rhythms of R&B music reinforced this desire to be in love. In my early twenties, I met the first woman with whom I felt I was truly in love. Suddenly the music and lyrics of my favorite songs connected meanings and impressions. I embraced so many new feelings and thoughts, and the experience was magical.

Since this was all new to me I was a bit naïve going into the relationship because this young woman had recently ended a tumultuous situation and was somewhat unsteady. We found comfort in one another, and after nearly a year of being friends, we began dating. We kept our circle of friends separate because her ex-boyfriend's network was still tightly connected to her. It did not matter to me because I had found what I thought was love after years of dreaming and imagining.

Twelve months into the relationship, I drove to her house late one evening and was surprised to see her ex-boyfriend's car parked in front of her place. My senses immediately heightened, and I began to physically shake. Then I knocked on the front door, which was opened by my half-asleep girlfriend. Blurting out my question about her ex-boyfriend's car, I felt my heart sink with her response. She was still in love with him and wanted to work things out. She had chosen not to tell me because she thought it would hurt me.

I pushed the memory out of my mind for sixteen years, never really addressing its impact until 2014 when I realized that since that time I had never developed a strong sense of trust with any woman that I dated. The mere thought of being cheated on created a physical sense of anxiety, very similar to that night sixteen years ago. Evidence of my lack of trust was clear because I always wanted to know about other relationships and plans.

Late in the summer of 2014 during a meditation, I came to a full awareness and definitive clarity. In this dream-like meditation, I witnessed every aspect of that night sixteen years ago. Rather than being the principle participant, I stood aside and observed our exchange at the front door. And as she closed the door, these words came to me, "David, it really has nothing to do with you."

I was not lacking; this was her choosing to suffer with this other love. Yet I had been lugging around an oversized boulder of unworthy-to-be-loved feelings, and they manifested in mistrust towards future relationships. That 2014 meditation experience was incredibly powerful, so much so that my sense of forgiveness, self-love, and esteem seemed to burst into an entirely new perspective overnight.

We have all witnessed friends, family, and coworkers choosing to continue relationships for many different reasons. There is a quote made famous in the movie *Jerry Maguire* when Tom Cruise emotionally says to Renee Zellweger, "You complete me." The movie script implies that both the character and moviegoers believe that wholeness only happens when we are enmeshed with another person. For years I subscribed to that false validation. However, becoming a parent to Lucia completely shifted my perceptions about giving and receiving love. This has been an awakening of immeasurable depth through which I now know that without loving and trusting myself it is almost impossible to love others and that practicing self-love is the ultimate form of true love. Now I feel self-contained and secure in the knowledge that true love radiates deep within me. And my ability to pour that love and loving-kindness into my environment and the world is the truest reflection of love for myself. We all are worthy and completely whole and always have been. We are perfectly who we are. Any perceptions of imperfections are misalignments. I hope that you are already moving toward that understanding and phenomenally grateful for it.

REIKI

The practice of Reiki originated in Japan as a technique for stress reduction, relaxation, and as a healing art. During a session a Reiki practitioner will lay their hands on or above the recipient to increase positive chi, or life force energy.

During or after a Reiki session, recipients and practitioners are likely to feel very relaxed, soothed, peaceful, glowing, and an overall sense of well-being. The physical body, mind, and spirit all benefit from this natural, safe healing art. As with massage and other therapeutic modalities, Reiki is often a complementary component of other treatments promoting recovery and accelerating well-being.

There is no specific belief system or religion attached to the practice of Reiki, however, it is spiritual in nature. Practitioners who have trained and practiced the breadth of Reiki teachings encourage personal self-improvement. For the practitioner the emphasis is on self-awareness; living in grace and gratitude goes far beyond an individual session and, indeed, is found across all cultures.

My friend Sean introduced me to a Reiki master named Susan, and I began studying with her in June 2013. The knowledge and practice of Reiki is an oral tradition passing from one master teacher to a student. Most Reiki master teachers feel very strongly about guiding their students through the levels, increasing self-awareness, and the importance of the relationship between practitioner and recipient. The results and benefits of a Reiki session are co-created by the intention of the recipient and the focus of the practitioner. Students of Reiki are taught about the importance of progressively raising their own vibrational frequency so that they will be able to pass Reiki energy on to others. Since my first Reiki class I have continued studying with Susan and will have achieved Reiki master level by summer 2015. After each session I feel vibrant, more alive, light, and free.

CHAPTER 10:
LETTERS OF APPRECIATION

"Appreciation is a wonderful thing. It makes what is
excellent in others belong to us as well."
—Voltaire

LETTERS OF APPRECIATION

Dear Jolie,

Thank you for the most beautiful gift of our daughter. I am confident that you are keeping your promise to raise Lucia in a home filled with love. My deep hope is that your heart will fill with compassion and you will be inspired to reunite Lucia and me once again. I miss and love her dearly and wish you well. Please know that my greatest desire is to be an active father to Lucia and to be with her as she grows up. Since I am experiencing the ache of losing her, I would never wish that on you, and I believe that we can both be in her life contributing to the strong foundation we dreamed of for her.

Peace and love,

David

Dear Mom and Dad,

My bond with both of you has grown significantly over the past few years. From the joy of Lucia's birth to the angst of her being taken away, I have felt your love. I couldn't be more proud of our connection. You have done so much to support me during one of the most challenging times of my life. Just a few weeks after the abduction, realizing how much I was hurting, you suggested that I move back in with you for as long as I wanted. I am so appreciative for that opportunity because it served as my lifeline to begin regrouping. You gave me space to grieve but were always close enough that I felt embraced by your positive and encouraging energy. Even though both of you have been hurt by these difficult circumstances, never once have you expressed disapproval or judgment toward Jolie or me. Your individual and collective compassion is remarkable, as is your sense of fairness and understanding. The family foundation that you laid out and nurtured is exemplary, and I will wholeheartedly follow it. It is my heartfelt desire to be able to demonstrate to you in small and large ways how deeply grateful I am for your love and support.

Peace and love,

David, aka Dee Jay

Dear Davida,

I couldn't have asked for a better sibling to experience life with. You are my rock and my rock star! I'm so proud of who you have become and to watch you grow as a leader in our family and in our community. Thank you for always allowing me to express who I want to be with an open heart and an open mind. My connection with you will last lifetime after lifetime.

Peace and love,

David, aka Dee Jay

Dear Aunt Varney,

When I think of you, and it is often, I imagine that you are seeing us with new eyes and smiling with pride as we continue our journeys and find our way. I am so glad for the many years with you and your constant encouragement to follow my passions. During the last ten years, I witnessed your struggles and wished with all my heart that I could have eased your discomforts. Today, I feel a sense of joy that you are at peace, no longer in pain. Your strength and courage and love for our family was always prominent. We continue to feel you in our hearts.

I miss you,

David, aka Dee Jay

Dear Family, Friends, and Colleagues,

I want to sincerely thank all of you for continuing to stand by my side. All of you—cousins, aunts, uncles, friends, and colleagues—have contributed to my healing (and thriving) ecosystem. By simply being open to new perspectives you have allowed me to be an example, and at times a role model, in your lives. My experience has become your experience, unfolding in beautiful ways. What I appreciate most about all of you is that even when we disagree, we never hurt one another. Love and respect reigns. For me, that is the definition of family, and I cannot thank you enough. Please know that you are always in my heart.

Peace and love,

David

Dear Otis, Jerrold, Darrell, Devon, Nick, Ricky, Archie, Donald, DP, and Vince,

My brothers, I thank you for always being supportive, even when times were extremely rough. Your collective compassion has inspired me to be authentically me. Thank you for allowing me to be both student and teacher in our relationships. I look forward to continuing to learn and grow together.

Peace and love,

David

Dear Erin, Sean, Michelle, Sophia, Margaret, Susan, and Maria,

You all are members of my "soul family." In very singular ways you have helped me understand spiritual experiences and profoundly encouraged me along new paths. Because of your guidance I have embraced and opened new and untapped gifts and ventured closer and closer to the "truest" me that I have ever known. Thank you for teaching me to allow and hold that sacred space. The unconditional love that you practice and have shared with me is like nothing I've ever felt. With each of you by my side, I've been invincible.

Erin, you've been the source that has brought each of these beautiful people into my life. Sean, you are the brother who took me under his wing to deepen my sense of connection to all that is. Michelle and Sophia, I'm appreciative of the years of coaching and mentoring that have guided me into deeper meditations and a stronger sense of my intuitive self. Margaret, your gifts need to be shared with the world! I am forever in your debt for the "GUIDE-ance" you have provided. Susan, you have introduced me to Reiki and the art of healing, which continue to blow me away each and every day. Maria, your light shines so bright! Your continued encouragement and support are the essence of who you are as a friend. Thank you all in the largest and most universal of ways!

Peace and love,

David

Dear Melissa,

From the first day that I met you there was such a strong sense of familiarity. It was as if we had known each other many lifetimes ago and we were reconnecting after a long absence. Thank you for being my friend and inspiring me from afar. It amazes me how just a few hours together and a car ride changed my life. Your level of openness has always stuck with me, helping to shape my expansion. Every single day your generous heart is open, and the truly special person that you are is evident in your zest for life, compassion, and authenticity. I urge you to always nourish your incredible light and the pride shining from your heart, fully aware that our world is richer because of your presence. I see the real you.

Peace and love,

David

Dear Joan,

Working with you for the past year has been a truly remarkable experience. Your coaching and editing methods have challenged me to expand as a writer and to tap into creative reservoirs of energy that I never knew existed. I am truly grateful that we have met and made this creative connection because this book would not be what it is without your support and belief in me.

Peace and love,

David

Dear Kickstarter Backers,

I want to sincerely thank Katherine Allen, Terry Ann Attaway, Donald and Davida Baker, Erik Braun, David and Anise Brown, Clifford Burns, Donna Cassetta, Ernest Choi, Megan Crawford, Karen Crouse, Mark Dalecki, Kimberly DeFilippi, Darrell Fincher, Robin Finerty, Rob and Olivia Glascock, Bryan Goshorn, Laura Hammons, Wiebke Heinrich, Von and Nicole Homer, Rima Hyder, Angela Jennings, Joseph and Tina Lamptey, Archie Leatherbury III, Anthea Lett, Jeff Loveland, Shayan Manzar, Erin McCloskey, Kristin Miller, Lauren Minter, Joanna Mongillo, Pauline Morgan-Riley, Therese Narzikul, Stephen Ovadje, Sean Palman, Donald, Marrisha and Victoria Pyle, Anne J. Ratledge, Donald Ratledge, Dorothy and Seana Rawlings, Cheris Reed, Jawara and Rachel Riley, William Riley, James "Trig" Rosseau, Dr. Roy Schutzengel, Nicole Simmons, Sheryl Sobiesiak, David and Amanda Stephens, Otis Stephens, Jerrold Taylor, Vincent Turner, Victoria Vlad, Charles Whitley, and Sharra Zagerman for supporting me throughout this journey. Many of you I have known for a long time, while some I've recently become acquainted with. Regardless of our relationship, without your compassion and support this project would not have come as far along as it has. Thank you for believing in me! I honor you for the special individuals that you are.

Peace and love,

David

Dear Reader,

Although I've taken a very intimate experience and put it out for the world to read, my hope is that you will be positively influenced as you read my reflections on awakening to gratitude in the midst of trauma. I believe that my closest friends and family have been impacted as much as I have by these experiences. In many ways writing this book has been a form of therapy for me. For my daughter, Lucia, I hope that it will introduce her to empathy and compassion for others and a real sense of how deeply I have missed being with her.

Vacillating between the highs and lows of our lives, we do our best to navigate the meandering curves and hair-pin turns of our day-to-day experiences, not unlike a roller coaster ride. If I asked you to describe the difference between a good and a bad experience, what would you say? Of course, there would be many different responses because *individual perspective* is the definitive ingredient.

We explore situations and scenarios in our minds. Then we spin definitions onto individual situations (people, places, things), which shapes our perspectives and the shading of "good" or "bad." Our perspectives are routed through and influenced by the many environments in which we live and work from birth through today and tomorrow. Our environments, and the people in them, become our teachers, so my point is that we learn as we go. We experience situations and express emotions that could rocket out of us or tunnel down into our deepest thoughts. Emotions are incredibly valuable and are often catalysts for deeper personal awareness and understanding. Most of us want to be engaged in doing things that feel "good," however, much of our time is spent preventing "bad" feelings or holding back, neither of which feel good. We allow our after-the-fact emotional kickbacks to define the goodness or badness of individual experiences. And for each one we are in charge of how we will define it. Consider this: all of these situations and emotional responses are fleeting and temporary. But the true secret, and it is really *not* a secret, to riding life's roller coasters in peace and joy lies in the perspectives we practice. As our lives unfold, one of the most phenomenal beauties is the ability to form our own perspectives and make choices in full awareness.

Choosing how to engage (or not) with personal emotions
Choosing the ways in which to respond
Choosing types of emotional energy to send out

You are the chooser of how you feel. Starting with this moment, do things differently and do different things. By sharing my story and the personal shift that I am experiencing, I hope that readers and everyone I come in contact with who may be coping with separation, loss, divorce, tragedy, or trauma will begin to consider clarity, calm, and peace as their new destinations.

Peace and love,

David Brown Jr.

P.S. I would like to hear from you. Nothing would bring me more joy than to know how I have encouraged someone just by sharing my journey. Please feel free to contact me through any of the methods below:

Website: www.davidbrownjunior.com
Email: david@davidbrownjunior.com
Facebook: www.facebook.com/davidbrownjunior
Twitter: @David_Brown_Jr